Bridges
in Understanding

Greta,

Thanks for being a supportive friend. Enjoy the read recognizing aboriginal humour & wisdom through story

Bridges in Understanding

Aboriginal Christian Men Tell Their Stories

Joyce Clouston Carlson
Alf Dumont, editors

ABC Publishing
ANGLICAN BOOK CENTRE

ABC Publishing
Anglican Book Centre
600 Jarvis Street
Toronto, Ontario M4Y 2J6

Royalties will be directed to Anglican and United Church healing funds.

Text typeset in Berkeley and Optima
Cover Art: Emily Carr, Untitled, c 1939, oil on canvas 91.3 X 65.7 cm, Vancouver Art Gallery, Emily Carr Trust, VAG 42.3.84 (Photo: Trevor Mills)
Art by Annette Loutit 1992.
From *The Dancing Sun: An Aboriginal Lent/Easter Resource*, published by the United Church of Canada, 1992. Used with permission.
Cover and text design by Jane Thornton

National Library of Canada Cataloguing in Publication

Bridges in understanding : Aboriginal Christian men tell their stories / Joyce Clouston Carlson and Alf Dumont, editors.

ISBN 1-55126-360-2
Printed in Canada

1. Native peoples—Canada—Religion. 2. Elders (Native peoples)—Canada—Biography. 3. Christian men—Canada—Biography. 4. McKay, Stanley. I. Carlson, Joyce II. Dumont, Alf

E78.C2B743 2003   248'.089'97071   C2003-900203-9

Contents

Foreword

Joyce Clouston Carlson

The vision for this publication emerged in the mid-eighties when the gifts of Aboriginal peoples became increasingly visible in churches; this was a time of tremendous political change in contemporary Canadian society. Among Aboriginal leaders promoting change within the church were graduates of theological colleges who had been nurtured and encouraged in their spiritual growth by Elders. The wisdom and integrity of Elders guided dramatic changes to church structures; however, historic undervaluing of oral traditions has meant that the spiritual gifts of these important contributors to our church life have been little known.

We are pleased to present the stories of five Elders to provide readers with a glimpse of their leadership and wisdom. These Elders are well loved; many have been involved politically in their communities as well as in their local and national churches. The separations between the spiritual and social dimensions of our lives — evident in much of Euro-based Canadian society and its education systems — is less arbitrary in Aboriginal communities, where spirituality openly infuses and informs social relationships. Elders bridge spiritual traditions, providing wisdom in churches and cross-cultural understanding in communities.

Bishop Andrew Atagotaaluk of Inuit heritage was born to a family in the high Arctic. Andrew's father taught him the skills necessary to live a traditional life on the land; his mother encouraged him in the Christian faith. His story traces the results of rapid breakdown of traditional culture in the last few decades; he shares his deep sense of the importance of identity in culture, and his vision to restore Inuit cultural values in the lives of children. In Andrew's view the person of Jesus transcends institutional boundaries.

The Rev. Arthur Ayoungman was the first Native person ordained in Alberta. His father was a traditional Siksika man, and his mother, who had been orphaned at the age of three, had been cared for by an Anglican priest and his wife, and was then placed in a boarding school at a very young age. Honoured with many names, Arthur's final name *Mais-toi-tsi-kin* had belonged to his great-grandfather, his spiritual mentor. Arthur married Nora, the daughter of a traditional holy woman; they supported their family of ten through farming and ranching. Arthur's athletic abilities, especially in hockey and horsemanship, and his success in rodeo competitions, are legendary. However, he was perhaps best known for his mediation skills at band council where he served for twenty-four years, for his honouring of the traditional Siksika values of sharing, and for his love of people. We are grateful to the members of Arthur's family, especially Vivian Ayoungman and Elaine Clifton, for contributing his story.

Burton Jacobs of Ojibway heritage shares his story in two parts. In the first, a poignant soliloquy, Burton documents his understanding of the personal strength required to overcome the obstacles he faced while serving as Chief of Walpole Island First Nation and leading his Nation to challenge the Indian agent's authority in his community. Walpole Island was the first Nation to declare self-government in 1969, and became a model for other Nations to develop different relationships with the Canadian government. In the second part of his story, Burton reflects on the process that led to the successful challenging of policies that failed to honour the spirit of original treaty agreements and undermined the health of their community. This story lends insight into the complex impact of colonial structures. We wish to thank Laverne Jacobs for contributing his father's story.

Murray Whetung of Ojibway heritage was born in Curve Lake, Ontario, near Peterborough. Soon after his marriage to Cobe, a teacher, Murray was posted overseas in the Canadian army. On returning, he worked as a mechanic and machine operator to support their family of thirteen children. Murray's willingness to learn from his children helped him understand the importance of affirming Native traditional ways. His deep acceptance and ability to use humour to guide and lead were gifts to his local United church and touched the lives of many in the All Native Circle Conference, of which he was a founding Leading Elder in the late eighties. In the early nineties, Murray responded to a call to the United Church ministry; he is now serving as a lay pastor in Alderville, Ontario.

Stanley McKay is Cree from Fisher River, Manitoba. A fisherman and trapper, Stanley was faced with rapid economic changes when overfishing by companies depleted fisheries, and wildlife habitat was destroyed by drainage of surrounding lands to promote farming. In the late fifties, Stanley moved with his family to Winnipeg in search of employment; he began working as a labourer in a candy factory, then was invited to become the first director of the Indian and Métis Reception Lodge, a United Church outreach ministry. Stanley calls for recognition of the profound differences between cultures, and demonstrates how to begin to bridge cultures. Scripture guides Stanley's understanding of life: *to do what is just, to show constant love, and to live in humble fellowship with God.* We are grateful to Stanley's wife, Verna, for assisting with Stanley's story.

This publication complements and is a companion to *Bridges in Spirituality: First Nations Christian Women Tell Their Stories* published in 1997. These books were inspired by the Rev. Dr. Alf Dumont, co-editor of this publication, and founding speaker of the All Native Circle Conference in the United Church of Canada; the Rev. Dr. Stan McKay, co-director of the Dr. Jessie Saulteaux Resource from 1988 to the present, and moderator of the United Church of Canada 1992 – 94; and the Rev. Canon Laverne Jacobs, serving as national staff with the Anglican Council of Indigenous Peoples in the Anglican Church of Canada from 1987 – 1996. All three of these men have held a variety of positions in their respective churches, and each had a dream of sharing with a larger audience stories that they had heard in sacred circles and meetings across Canada. My social work career in Winnipeg, the city with the largest urban Aboriginal population in Canada, led me to an awareness of the centrality of spirituality for families dealing with rapid social change and displacement. Together we began to explore how to affirm and nurture spirituality in Aboriginal communities, as well as provide ways for the larger church to support this growth; we believed an important beginning was through sharing spiritual stories.

Capturing the voice and honouring the intent of stories from an Aboriginal worldview in words and publications based on Euro-Canadian values has been challenging. That we are all of First Nations or Métis heritage[1] and were born in rural commu-

---

1. A note on terminology: The Royal Commission on Aboriginal Peoples (1996) used the term *Aboriginal* to refer to political and cultural groups original to North America. The term *First Nations* refers to persons who belong to communities that entered into formal treaty relationships under the "Indian Act" with the Canadian Government. Métis persons are of mixed First Nations and European background and historically did not enter treaty agreements with the Canadian government; Métis children did not usually attend residential schools. The term *Inuit* replaces the former term *Eskimo* (*Royal Commission on Aboriginal Peoples*, 1996, vol. 1, xiv–xv). The term *Native* is sometimes used interchangeably with *Aboriginal*.

nities meant that we had each negotiated a personal path between the values of our familes and those of urban Canadian educational structures. Our shared committment to the importance of stories led to formation of the First Nations Ecumenical Liturgical Resources Board. This enabled drawing on our collective skills and training in theology, education, business, and social work to experiment with publications. When board members moved on to different places in their careers, Alf and I continued working to bring the dream to completion in two final publications focussing specifically on lives of Elders. The spirit of the original board lives on in this volume through inclusion of Burton Jacobs and Stanley McKay, fathers of Laverne and Stan. We are grateful to Laverne for assisting with his father's and Andrew's stories, and for Stan's consultation in his father's story.

These stories will be appreciated by all persons with a keen interest in spirituality, as well as educators and professionals working in systems that bring cultures together, such as schools and social service agencies. They are symbolic of many stories from a rich heritage. Our hope is that others will continue to find ways to write and share stories that, to now, have been held in the minds and memories of gifted community members. We commend this publication especially to children and families whose heritage is connected to Elders they may never meet, as well as to all those who may not have experienced firsthand the wisdom, laughter, and joy of the Elders.

Elders

Alf Dumont

Being an Elder is a profound responsibility. Through their wisdom, gentle spirit, humour, faith, and deep spirituality, the Elders lead us. We are always given the opportunity to learn. When we do not make good use of our opportunities, the Elders feel the pain. They know that if the teachings that come through them and their stories are not received, they have failed in their responsibility to care for seven generations after them and to take responsibility for seven generations before them. We who listen are *potential Elders*, or as some of us have said, "Elders in training … training is for a lifetime."

Elders learn at the feet of other Elders whom they have honoured and respected. Elders are guided from the *spirit world* through dreams and visions. Prayer is the way of life. Humility is the road to be walked.

There are many Elders in the world. Each has profound and deep teachings to share, and we can learn from all of them. However, not all Elders will be our personal teachers and guides. One Elder told my brother Jim, "Do not have too many Elders. You will become confused." All Elders, however, must be honoured and respected. We need to listen to their stories and teachings, for they have much to share with us.

In this book are many stories and many teachings. There is great wisdom and humour. Read carefully. Listen well. Hear the spirit speaking. As a reader you may wonder at certain stories. You may say, "What does this teach me? I don't get it." Often we who listen do not understand. Our responsibility is to carry the teaching carefully around with us until we do. So, if the story does not speak to you or doesn't make sense, live with it and you will find that in time there will be a teaching. If we have carried the story carefully, it means that we have unfolded parts of its teachings and have applied what we can to our way of living and being. If we have not carried the story carefully, then when the Elder sees us doing things the same way we always did, the Elder might ask, "Do you remember the story I told you? Do you remember what you have been taught?"

In the First Nations community we learn to listen differently. I remember when I was at a gathering of the All Native Circle Conference. We were embroiled in a heated debate about what had happened in one community. We could not agree on what direction to take. We broke for dinner, and afterward we went on discussing other issues. As the next days passed, we did not return to the issues about that community. On the third day, while we were in the midst of talking about educational matters, one Elder arose and spoke. After several minutes, most of us understood that he had returned to the discussion we had had three days ago about what happened in that certain community. Having thought about it for a long time, the Elder was now ready to offer a teaching or tell a story that would be of help to those people from that community. It did not matter that the advice came when it did, but that the advice was offered and the people were there to hear it. Some of our non-Aboriginal colleagues did not understand what was happening and why the Elder was not speaking to the point at hand. But he *was* speaking to the point at hand, for in his mind we had never left the other conversation, and the teachings were helpful to those who needed them. There is a great difference in the way First Nations people and non-First Nations people think and work.

Cliff Tewiyaka, a Sioux tradition teacher from the Standing Buffalo community in Saskatchewan, once told me the story of a small group in South Dakota who had called in an Elder to teach them the sacred ways. The old man came and agreed to stay for one week. In that week he did not show them how to make a lodge or prepare for ceremonies. He told them story after story. He told them jokes and made them laugh. They were disappointed, even though they enjoyed their time with the old man. They asked him to stay on for another week. He agreed. He told them more stories and more jokes. Then he left. They were even more disappointed. Then they began to repeat the jokes and the stories with each other. After a long time of sharing these stories, they began to realize that he had told them everything they needed to know. They had everything they needed to begin the recovery of their traditional teachings.

Read well. Listen carefully to the Elders as they tell their stories in their own way.

Acknowledgements

We wish to express our deep appreciation to the Elders and their families who shared their lives and their time to enable these stories to be published. We are grateful to a number of funders who have trusted our process and shared their resources generously:

Bay of Quinte Conference
Bay of Quinte United Church Women
Diocese of Rupert's Land
Division of Mission, United Church of Canada
The Healing Fund, United Church of Canada
Faith, Worship and Ministry Committee, Anglican Church of Canada
Fellowship of the Maple Leaf, United Kingdom
Regent's Park United Church Foundation, Winnipeg
St. James Westminster Church Foundation, Huron Diocese
St. Stephen's Broadway United Church Foundation, Winnipeg
Westennial United Church Foundation, Toronto

Special thanks to the diocese of Rupert's Land, which has provided a "home" for the project over a period of years. Carol Throp was instrumental in encouraging initial funding. Cathy Mondor assisted with the word processing for Stanley McKay's manuscript.

Karen Stuart and Chris Salstrom assisted with project management. Bishop Walter Jones provided practical encouragement at the inception of the Liturgical Resources Board, and Bishop Pat Lee provided ongoing support. The Rev. Phyllis Keeper has been a constant friend.

We are grateful to our colleagues in the national churches and at the Child Guidance Clinic of Winnipeg for their support and encouragement over the decade of the project's life. St. John's United Church in Alliston, Ontario, encouraged Alf and his family, and St. Margaret's Anglican in Winnipeg was spiritually nurturing of Joyce and her family as the projects unfolded. Dr. Mac Watts of Winnipeg and Richard Chambers of Toronto were helpful while the project was beginning, and Leyah McFadyen has been a friend throughout. We would like to thank our two colleagues who have journeyed with us throughout the process and were part of the Liturgical Resources Board: the Very Rev. Dr. Stanley McKay and the Rev. Canon Laverne Jacobs. We thank our families: Barb, Mike, and Dan Dumont; Len and Andrea Carlson, Ian Sunabacka, Karen Sunabacka, and Preston Parsons for supporting the vision, and occasionally overlooking absences; Robert Maclennan for sensitively shepherding these stories to publication, and Greig Dunn for skilful editing.

The Great Creator whose love transcends divisions in our lives, families, and communities has been central to the vision in all publications. All stories are used by permission of the storytellers; their trust and willingness to share are a great to all of us. With wonderful grace, our lives have been enriched by opportunities to work creatively together, with the First Nations Board, and with Elders and their families.

Joyce & Alf

Soliloquy: Who Am I?

Burton Jacobs

Who am I?

Am I an Indian standing alone, undecided — hoping, waiting for an opportunity to come?

If that is so, I may wait forever. Opportunity comes only to those who make it.

Who am I?

Am I an Indian who has been unjustly treated, and have I in return unjustly hated?

Goodness knows I've had more than my share of trouble.

But does it serve any useful purpose to constantly dwell on my misfortunes?

I know that hatred hurts only me — not the people I hate.

Yet after all these years, I am still bitter and hateful.

Why? Why do I hate?

Can it be that I do not understand myself — my state of oneness with God and humanity and all living creatures — and the nature of hatred?

Thus it follows that —

when I hate, I also hate myself;

when I destroy, I also destroy myself;

when I kill, I also kill a part of myself.

All life is interrelated. You cannot destroy a part of it without damaging the whole.

Who am I?

Part of humanity and of every living creature, as I have been taught by Indian religion.

Then all humanity are my brothers and sisters, whether they be red, white, or black.

We are all children of the same Father.

We all have the same likeness, the same hopes, the same tears, the same desire for praise, the same desire for love, the same desire to live, and the same longing for happiness.

Why then should I mistreat and hate my own family?

Membership in the human family includes the difficult responsibility of keeping myself straight and upright. Without first keeping my own life in a respectable order, I cannot rightfully expect any good to come from others.

Membership in the human family accords me the right to live as others do and to be treated as an equal. I have the same right to pursue the kind of life I want to live. I have the same desire to work — to keep me from need. I also have the same desire to assume the responsibility that my living imposes upon me. But I must always remember that brotherhood has an unwritten law, which decrees that whatever rights and privileges I assume, they must be exercised within prescribed limits of order.

Who am I?

Am I the strong man that I think I am?

Am I strong enough to conquer myself?

Have I strength enough to subdue my weakness of will — the temptation to play with drugs and alcohol like a child?

Have I enough resistance to keep me from lying, cheating, or stealing?

Do I have enough moral strength to always stand for what is right?

This is the enemy within, whom I must conquer in order that I may not go astray.

There are other enemies from without, who will always take advantage of my weakness and my unguarded moments. Their poisoned words, written or spoken, fester in the mind to make it sick.

Likewise, the ghosts of many broken treaties long since dead have always haunted and tormented me. Yet I know very well that these ghosts are without substance. Still I see them grinning on my bookshelf at night. They follow me wherever I go. When I take long flights across the country to attend Indian meetings, I see them there.

I must not allow these frightening visions to break my spirit.

When this happens I fall apart.

I lose hope.

I feel defeated.

I lose control.

Then I begin to skid — downward.

There is a danger that, after fighting these elusive ghosts for several lifetimes, I may extract from them no more than a handful of beads, a few blankets, some gun powder, and perhaps a barrel of whiskey.

I hope I am strong enough to recover from such bitter disappointments. I hope I can emerge from them a wiser stronger man.

Who am I?

Am I a human being with all the intelligence and capabilities required to accomplish anything that can be accomplished?

Can I climb heights that hitherto have never been reached?

Can I achieve anything that I set my heart to?

Have I been given the will and the untiring spirit to pursue my goal?

Have I been endowed with talents that I never knew I had?

If our Maker created all men equally, then surely I too must have the latent ability to accomplish some meaningful sustaining work — work that lifts my spirits and makes me a proud and confident man.

Who am I?

Am I bigger than myself?

Am I broad-minded enough not to consider every irregular act as an act of discrimination?

Am I mature enough to take the slights or practical jokes that men and women play?

Am I responsive enough to those who want to talk with me and befriend me?

Am I strong enough to speak out against the abuses of Native rights and treaties?

Indian treaties have been used to cloak and to conceal those who want to operate outside the law. I hope I am big enough to stop such outrageous acts of trickery, whether committed by Indian or white.

No people can for long retain credibility or respect when it falsely uses its noble causes to gain public sympathy.

Who am I?

Am I sensible enough to know that gifts or money or development programs are not enough to make me strong?

The making of myself must come from within.

Who am I?

Am I determined enough to rise above myself and overcome the many obstacles that lie across my pathway?

Who am I?
Am I bigger than myself?
Am I —
An Indian?
A Canadian?
A North American?
Or one who is of the whole earth?

Andrew Atagotaaluk

with Laverne Jacobs
and Robert Maclennan

*When God calls me,
he is calling me
as an Inuk person;
he's not trying to move me
into another culture.*

Recalling family history

I'll begin from where I start remembering my life as a hunter's son. We were always out on the land. That's where I learned my skills of survival. My family travelled around a lot in search of where the game was most sufficient. I've never had the experience of being in a large community. In the late fifties and early sixties, we were still living off the land. I rarely remember going into a trading post.

My situation was different from most people's because my grandparents died before I was old enough to even remember them. I knew my mother's mother, but she died when I was very small. My mother shared some stories with us about the way people used to live. I think her mother — my grandmother — lived at the time when Christianity came. It was also a time when the whalers came. So she lived when Inuit and European culture were already mixing. My grandmother's father was a whaler. He knew the old way of hunting humpback whales, and so the white whalers wanted him to work for them.

When my mother was growing up, there was prejudice against her, and kids would pick on her because her parents were separated and she was part white in appearance. She had a rough time, and sometimes this showed in the way she behaved towards us. My dad had his own hurts and pains. His parents had died when he was very small, and he had been adopted. Then his first wife and their four children all died in a big epidemic in 1948, and he had to bury them all himself.

My dad wouldn't tell us how to do things, but he would let us watch him. That's how we learned how to make a sled, how to hunt for caribou or walrus, and how to fish. He didn't say how much he loved us, but he showed it by the way he looked after us and trained us. It looked harsh, but it was very good.

My father liked to be alone. I remember arriving home from school in the plane one year with my sister and finding that our parents had gone down to the Hudson's Bay Company post at Spence Bay. They had left a message with another family at the camp asking them to look after us if we arrived before they got back. Two weeks later we saw a dog team and sleds coming down the bay, and we knew it was our parents. But they didn't come into the camp. They stopped at a little island and set up their own camp there. I was really disappointed, but that's the way my father was. If he didn't want to be with other people, he wouldn't come into a camp no matter who was waiting. I guess he carried many hurts in his heart, and in those days nobody talked about personal stuff the way we do nowdays. There were no healing circles, and nobody could identify why a person behaved in a certain way. He was very touched when he saw a poor kid with torn clothes. I guess it reminded him of when he was young and wasn't properly looked after, and I guess it affected the way he behaved as a man.

Recalling traditional spirituality

My knowledge of what Inuit used to believe was passed on to me by my mother, but even in her time the old beliefs were no longer part of people's lives. Life was difficult then and, in English terms, nomadic. You needed other people's help. From hardship people learned to have a generous feeling towards others. That's how the sharing custom of Inuit people developed. Just about everybody lost relatives from starvation, and that kind of difficulty makes people look beyond themselves and become more compassionate towards others.

You had to believe in the supernatural in order to have not just the physical ability to survive but also the power to live. You needed more than your own knowledge and skills.

You needed the help of a higher power. And there is assistance — a spiritual side of you that can help you.

That's how I think shamanism began. I use the word shamanism because that's what people understand, but in Inuktitut the word is *anakok*. There's no equivalent in English. An anakok or shaman could control dark powers. Our stories show there were two kinds of shamans: those on the dark side and those on the bright side. The good ones could help a person who was spiritually attacked by this dark power.

I remember when the Americans first put a man on the moon. That was the first time we heard news from the south on the radio. The announcer was talking excitedly to an old man who was a Native person, saying, "The Americans have landed on the moon. It's something like a miracle, isn't it?" The old man wasn't excited. He just said, "Oh, yeah. We used to be there." He was referring to the shamans who knew how to travel to the spirit realms.

From what I can gather, the shamans lived by their own rules and were different from the rest of the people. They were associated with foxes, wolves, whales, and polar bears, and the more experienced they became and the more spirits they had, the more powerful they were. A shaman once told me, "It's very lonely to be a shaman because you have your own rules, and if you don't follow them, the spirit will be unhappy with you and you won't be able to work according to your wishes. You have to live by the right rules because of having that kind of relationship with the spirit." It was almost like the Old Testament prophets.

All the people had to live according to the rules the shaman set. This was connected with what the white man calls superstition. For instance, if the people were short of food and were having a hard time finding animals, the shaman would meditate to find out who had broken the sacred rules and was responsible for the problem. When somebody came forward and admitted that they had broken the rules, the transgression was corrected and everything went back to normal.

The shaman wasn't necessarily the leader of the community, but he was the one who could advise on anything beyond the visible. He was in charge of knowing the reasons for things that lie beyond human abilities. Let's say a family is having difficulty getting seal, so they're short of oil and meat and food for the dogs. Somebody must have done something against the rules. So the Elder in the camp goes to the shaman and asks him to find out. But the shaman doesn't work just on request. He has to be paid. Maybe the man gives him a harpoon head or a whip. Then the shaman goes to work.

I know a story about a woman whose husband had gone out hunting with another man. The other man came back alone and said that her husband had been drowned. It was during that time of the year when the ice is just forming and you can't trust it to walk on. The woman accepted the explanation, but she was unsatisfied. Later — years or months, I don't know — much later she went to a shaman she trusted, gave him her ulu (her woman's knife) and an ornament, and asked, "Would it be possible for you to find out what really happened to my husband?" The shaman went alone into his tent, and by a trance or whatever practice he did, he tracked down two men walking towards a herd of caribou. Apparently the man who came back alone had something against the woman's husband because he shot him from behind. He told the woman, who finally learned what had really happened to her husband.

These were some of the capabilities shamans had, but not all shamans were the same. There are stories going around that they were able to heal, or cure someone who had a sickness that nobody understood, or bring back to life someone who had accidentally died. Sometimes they had the ability to provide an animal for a family that needed one for meat, like bringing a seal to a place where seal are rarely found.

There were many other rules that had to be strictly obeyed because, otherwise, something bad would happen to the whole clan or camp. For instance, if a woman was pregnant, she had to live alone. They made a little tent for her, and the husband was not allowed to see her until she had given birth. After the birth she had to spend another three days alone, and only a woman could give her what she had to eat. Only then could she be reunited with her husband. My grandmother used to say that it was very difficult, and sometimes fearful, because you had to really respect the rules that were set for the whole camp.

Early years

When a lot of the Inuit people were affected by tuberculosis, they were taken south and some never returned. Some who did return didn't survive very long. Every year families would go down to the Hudson's Bay Company post and have their x-ray done. My grandmother was affected, and because my older brother lived with her, the doctors thought he might be affected. So they both went down south in a small yellow plane that I dreamed about afterward. I don't really remember my brother. I only know about him from what my mother told me. My parents had adopted another boy named Simon, whose father had also died of tuberculosis, and I thought he was my real brother.

When my grandmother came back alone, she said, "I left Tony. They said he has to go to school." My brother was only about six when he was taken away from my grandmother and sent to a boarding school. I think my mother inquired through administrators, and they found him in a small boarding school outside Edmonton. When he came back, he was about eleven, and he didn't speak a word of his native language. He was like a stranger even though he was our blood brother. We couldn't communicate with him, but they brought along a translator. It was strange: we didn't know how to talk to him and he didn't know how to talk to us. I guess he had got used to living in a different environment. He had never seen a wooden building before because we had lived in an igloo in the winter and in a sod hut in the summer. He quickly picked up our language, but it was hard for him. To us it seemed natural that a person who had lived for a long time in the south would not be familiar with our language and the way we lived.

The year my brother came home, all the children from other camps went to school, but the government said they would make an exception for us because our brother needed company to get used to the environment and family setting. So it wasn't until the following year that I went out to school for the first time. It was very difficult for my parents and for me. As children we were never away from our parents for long for any reason. We knew other children, but the camps where we all lived were scattered along the coast of the central Arctic, so we weren't together with other children much.

The first year at school was very difficult. I woke up crying, not knowing where I was. But you have to adapt. Fortunately there were some boys from a nearby camp, so they were like relatives even though we were not related. And we got to know children from other parts of the Arctic. Gradually we got used to the place. Seeing a building two storeys high for the first time was awesome. Cars and roads and trees were things we'd never known were in the same world. It made you feel small to be in a completely different world. But we adapted.

Our parents didn't understand English education and why we had to be in school or even whether they should support us. They just knew it had to be done. They had no choice. That's the message they received from the government. At the time they didn't show that they were upset in front of their children; that's part of our custom. So we didn't know until much later, when they started to talk about the experience, how difficult it had been for them. My mother said she couldn't hold back her tears, and that's why she had turned away. It was very difficult for the parents because they didn't know the people who were going to look after us or whether they would look after us well.

During my school days when I was away for eight months of the year, I would forget my Inuktitut, but since I was nine by the time I went away to school, the language would come back when I returned home.

Looking back, I think everything has a benefit if you look at it from the positive side, even if it has damaged you. When we later expressed the hurt and shared it with our parents, that helped to compensate for what might have been. And later we saw how we had benefited from the school. Without it I wouldn't have been involved with the church or accomplished many of the things I have.

When I was about seventeen, in 1967, my older brother (the one who had gone to school before me) went to Resolute to work, and all my other brothers and sisters were away at school. My parents said, "You have to stay home this year because your father is going to need an extra hand." The government said I was old enough to make up my own mind, so from then on I never went back to school.

Christianity and traditional culture

Staying home and helping my father to run the camp let me get to know the culture. We lived off the land all the time, hunting and getting our food, making our own dwellings.

At school I had got used to being around my peers and classmates and the authorities. When I decided not to go back, I was very lonely because my brothers and sisters, except for the youngest sisters, were away at school and my older brothers all had jobs at Resolute. This was the age when you're beginning to be interested in the opposite sex. We used to go to trade at Spence Bay until we discovered Resolute was much closer by dog team. At Resolute I met Mary, and the following year I moved there. Before long Mary and I got married.

It was a big change. I had come from such a quiet place, but in Resolute there were TVs, radios, and men learning how to work at jobs. The US Air Force had set up an air base at Resolute, and the Canadian government wanted to establish its sovereignty by having an Inuit community living there because at that time nobody lived permanently in that part of the Arctic. So families were relocated to Resolute from northern Quebec. Mary's family was one of them. It was very hard for these people, but only later did the relocation become a human rights issue. The people had to start a new life, and they had to get used to a life of going to work every day. Alcohol was available and heavy drinking started.

A minister used to visit twice a year from Pond Inlet. He noticed that I was capable of helping in the church. My mother was brought up as a Christian, and she had a lot of influence on me. I had been baptized in the Anglican Church, and she had encouraged me to grow up in the Christian way. Even by the time I was born, the Inuit had already lost most of their old beliefs and Christianity had already spread across the Arctic, so I grew up not knowing about our own spirituality.

Coming off the land, I had never really been associated with the institutional church and I wasn't familiar with its customs, but when the Pond Inlet minister asked, I agreed to help. At that time I was not used to leading people. This was my starting point, but I felt I didn't know enough. I wanted to know the Bible more. The next year there was going to be an evangelical mission in the high Arctic, and the minister said that because I was young and able to speak English and was already involved with the church, I could be a translator for the evangelists.

I made my decision on the day of the evangelistic mission. Until then I understood Jesus Christ only as a story in the Bible. My mother had told me to read the Bible every day, and I tried to read it in Inuktitut, but because of my schooling, my Inuktitut reading wasn't very good, so I read it mostly in English. At that service Jesus Christ became for the first time a real person in my life. I realized that he was my saviour and lord, and I had been ignoring him.

From then on I wanted to deepen my understanding. The bishop told me they had opened a theological training centre in Pangnirtung. I felt I should go there because God was calling me to the ordained ministry. Although my wife and I were very young, we decided together that we would go.

As I became older and my knowledge began to deepen a little bit, I began to realize that Jesus is a God person, but he also has respect for all the kinds of people in the world. I started to sense that I was not really presenting Christ as an Inuk. I was presenting him more like a white person. I started to realize that I had to believe in Jesus as an Inuk and do things the way he did, but in an Inuit way. It isn't enough to present Jesus as the truth and the way. You have to take culture into account as well. That's the way he presented himself.

At the same time I started to realize that most of my culture was gone. My language was near extinction. It was very hard for my people to get used to dealing with a large community setting, to learn how to respect each other, and to deal with the education and court systems. They were having problems with family, alcohol, suicide, sexual abuse, and lack of jobs. Why? The problem is loss of identity. My people didn't know who they were anymore, and they didn't really care what happened to them. The old people, who knew better, had gone silent. The young people, who have taken on the new life, are also lost in it.

And I began to see that when God calls me, he is calling me as an Inuk person; he's not trying to move me into another culture. I still have to survive in the way my ancestors survived, because it's the only way you can live in the Arctic, even though we have modern transportation and so on. It's essential for you to be who you are, in your own culture and language, and God loves and respects you for that.

I'm a bishop, but I know that the church brought some of the problems. For example, the Anglicans and Roman Catholics would both come to the same place, and soon the Inuit realized that, in the name of doing good, the churches were dividing people. It would have been okay if the preachers had just said that Jesus is the saviour who brings eternal life. But their message came as part of a package that included regulations and policies. Take meetings, for example. White people have an agenda. When Inuit gather, they don't have an agenda. It's good to have an agenda, and you can get used to it, but when you adapt like that, you're not really respecting your own way of doing things. We're still taking in the way the white people do things and thinking it's the best way.

St. Paul's story helps to explain what went wrong and how it can be different. When he went out as a Pharisee representing an institution, he saw people as enemies. But when Jesus appeared to him on the road, Jesus spoke to him as a person: "Paul, Paul, why are you hurting me?" So Paul realized that all the boundaries that he thought important were garbage. The missionaries should have presented Jesus as a person who speaks to persons, not as an institutional package. Pure Christianity is very similar to what our ancestors taught: respect life and never abuse it. Never abuse an animal or a person or a relationship. By respecting God you respect your own life and the life of other people.

Most Inuit are Christians. As Christians it's our responsibility to care for each other as people. In the future, I think Inuit are going to be guided by a new vision. We're going to become more self-sufficient and more unified. We're going to believe more in ourselves. We're going to set our own goals and make them happen. We're going to take control over our lives and find solutions to our own problems. Through our own vision, we'll restore what has been lost, including the traditional knowledge. Already we have programs to teach young people how to survive on the land, and we want kids to be able to get school credits for what they learn of the old ways, so they won't feel that learning to build an igloo, for example, is a waste of time. So I think there is hope.

Murray Whetung

with Alf Dumont

Growing up on the reserve

From the moment of birth, an Aboriginal person is an esteemed member of both a family and a nation. Murray Whetung was born on 30 November 1921 into the Ojibwa nation on the Mud Lake Reserve near Peterborough, Ontario. (Mud Lake has since been renamed Curve Lake). His parents, Daniel Eli and Muriel, had two other sons, Floyd and Clifford, and they had adopted their niece Marjorie, who was the oldest of the four. The community was made up of about two hundred and fifty to three hundred people.

As a child, Murray was free to do what he wanted. His mother did not see him from morning till dark in the summertime. He and his friends caught fish, black birds, and squirrels, skinned or scaled them, then boiled them all in a pail for lunch down by the lake. They were very independent.

> Sometimes the older men would take the young guys out fishing and trapping. You learned a lot of things from them. They would teach us how to hunt muskrat or catch muskees by hitting them with a paddle. You had to be quick.
>
> We also learned how to collect birch bark without killing the tree. The old people taught us always to say a little prayer and thank God for supplying the birch bark on the trees. Sometimes they would leave a little tobacco as part of the prayer. Even though they were devoted in the Christian way, they had not forgotten many of the traditional ways of respect for the Creator and the creation. The teaching was always practical, and it was also shown through the way of life, the way of living. You didn't notice. It was just there.
>
> The old women, the grandmothers in the community, were strong. If they saw you doing something that you weren't supposed to do, they would tell you what you had done and tell you why it was wrong. This was especially true of anything done around the church and how you behaved in church.

We always went to church. We were expected to but never forced to. We learned from our parents and from others in the community to respect what others believe and hold as important for them. This way I could walk in life respecting the traditional ways of the Ojibwa people, the ways of the United Church, and the Mormon ways of my wife, Cobe.

The old people also taught us that there were many people who carried on bad medicine. We were told to stay away from them because they knew how to do you harm. But most walked in a good way. Some spiritual people used the shaking tent. Some did not need a shaking tent, like the old man who just lit a fire and lay down beside it and received visions and messages. He and a group of men were up at the logging camp north of Curve Lake. Two of them followed the old man one night to where he lit the fire. Next morning he had news of what was happening back home. Many people could travel in this way. The Ojibway term for it is *jiiskee*.

The Elders taught as much by example as by precept.

One beautiful night when I was about nine years old, I went out skating. I skated until I came to the shore and found a stump that I thought would be good for a bonfire. I pushed it across the lake, but when I got tired, I put it behind a tree near the edge that marked the way to cross the lake. We usually had to work in the store until about eight o'clock in the evening when it closed, and one night soon after, Dad let my brother Clifford, who was twelve, drive his Model T Ford to the lake. We drove right across to where there was a bonfire.

When we were about to leave, some of the guys at the bonfire jumped on the back and began to push the car around, and Clifford drove through some bushes to knock them off. I saw my stump and yelled, "That's not a bush, that's a stump!" It was too late. We hit the stump, and it flew up and dented the hood. We kept on driving until we came home. Dad wasn't angry. Next morning he just went back into the bush where he had some old Model T's and found another hood.

Murray attended the Mud Lake day school. Two further years at the continuation school gave him a year's credit at Peterborough Collegiate Vocational School, so he started there in Grade 10. After graduating in 1938 he held a series of jobs: with his father, in logging camps, at a feed mill, at General Electric in Peterborough, in construction, and picking peaches in Niagara.

The war years

After Murray returned home from Niagara, he tried to join the air force, but having heard nothing from them, in August 1942, he decided to join the army.

> I finished my basic training in Peterborough, where they had built an army camp in the exhibition grounds. Then they shipped us off to Kingston to do advanced training. In November I got a telegram to report for duty at Manning Pool in Toronto, where they recruited air force personnel. But my commanding officer said, "You may not realize it, but you are not available for any further recruiting." So I stayed in the army.
>
> While I was there, they were recruiting for guys to be wireless operators. However, it was well known that if you got to be a wireless operator, you would most likely be in the tail of a bomber as a gunner. And it was also well known that many of those in the tail section got killed. They gave us tests to see if we could do Morse Code. I tried to fail, because I did not want the job in the tail section, but I almost passed! Still, they let me go, and I stayed on as a lineman, whose duties were to build and repair telephone lines.

In 1943, Murray married. His wife, Elva, an Ojibway like himself, was a teacher.

> She made me feel good about my work even though I was never a real money-maker. And she did such a good job of bringing up our children.

Everyone called her Cobe — short for *Aancobgigun*, which means "tying the generations together" — as with ropes. She was given the name because she was the fifth-generation daughter: the first girl to be born, and the oldest of her family of the fifth generation. The name was a teaching; in Ojibway tradition, all names are teachings, describing who we are and how we are to live our lives. Cobe carried that teaching all her life and lived up to its responsibility.

> We could communicate without speaking. One day I left to take a cow to Guelph. After I left, Elva said to her sister Ida that she could get me to bring home whatever she wanted. Ida responded, "Well, get him to bring something nice." On the way home I bought some beautiful gladiolas at a farmer's roadside stand. When I brought the flowers into the house, I noticed a look that passed between the two women. The look said, "I told you so."
>
> Cobe and I did not have our own home, so we stayed with Cobe's grandmother.

Shortly after the marriage, Murray was sent overseas with the army as part of the signal corps. Since someone had developed scarlet fever on the boat to England, the men were quarantined and spent lots of time in camp with nothing to do except learn precision marching.

> We went into France in June 1944 just before D-Day [the day the Allied forces landed in France to begin the offensive that

led to their eventual victory] to lay underground cable from the beach at Caen. I was one of the truck drivers. When we set off inland, we were lost for most of the night because the captain couldn't read a map. We finally ended up back where we began, and the captain commanded us to dig a trench to sleep in. But I rigged up a hammock in the truck. In the middle of the night we were awakened by a deep booming sound. The sound got louder and louder. Finally, stumbling in my sleepiness, I discovered that one of our big seventeen-inch guns was firing over the truck where I was trying to sleep.

To lay the cable they had to hollow out the trenches by hand because there was no heavy equipment to dig with. Later, the army brought in two bulldozers. The cables were supposed to run as far as Brussels, but just when they thought their work was done, the men were moved to a different location to lay more cable. During this operation, the five men stayed at a hotel run by a Frau Walker, who treated them royally. Even when the army rolled in and suddenly there were forty or fifty soldiers to feed, Frau Walker wouldn't let the army cook do his job. She insisted on doing all the cooking, and she traded rations for booze to bribe him to keep out of her way. He had to be sent away to dry out.

During the war one of the men used to write to his mother every week. He was very good about this. But suddenly she stopped receiving letters. She went to a man who was able to travel in the spirit world. He told her that her son had a long cut on his back. He had ducked down to crawl under a wire, and a sniper's bullet tore through his flesh and made a scar about eighteen-inches-long. If he had been standing, he would have died. She was grateful for the message. When he came back from the war, he did have a scar about eighteen-inches long down his back.

Back home: Tradition renewed

It wasn't until November 1945 that Murray finally returned home. He worked as a mechanic for fifteen years, then as a machine operator in a factory making parts for lawn mowers, outboards, and skidoos until he retired at age sixty-one in 1982.

Murray and Cobe have thirteen children, twenty-seven grand-children, and three great-grandchildren. Their children, encouraged and supported by their parents, followed their own callings and became teachers, construction workers, homemakers, maintenance workers, store owners, health workers, nurses, and directors of halfway houses and day-care centres. In their spiritual journeys, too, they followed their own hearts. For some it was the teachings from the Mediwiwin Lodge of the Ojibwa, the Sioux teachings of the Sundance, the teachings of the Chiapas of Mexico; for others it was the Roman Catholic and Protestant traditions, the Mormon Church; and for still others it was their own ways and understandings. Cobe and Murray respected them and their choices, and they in turn respected their father and mother in the decisions they made. Respect is a core teaching in the traditional sacred way.

As an Elder back home on the reserve at Curve Lake, Murray always worked to keep alive both the traditional way and the Christian way.

> Once a group of young men made a drum, and I made a place for them on my property. I used to sit with them while they played or listen to them from the house, but my neighbour, the chief, thought they were drumming up bad spirits and should be stopped. They had to move the drum to where the chief couldn't hear them.

Another group of young men brought to Murray a drum that they had made, gave him an offering of tobacco, and asked him to name the drum. They didn't expect an immediate response, and Murray went away and prayed to have insight. It took about a month until a name was given to him from the spirit world: *nimkii en wed* — voice of thunder.

Becoming involved in the church

Between 1979 and 1982, Murray became more involved at the Curve Lake United Church. He was asked to take over the senior Sunday school program. In 1983 he joined the National Consultations of Native People, and later he was selected, along with Gladys Taylor, to be one of the two Leading Elders of the All Native Circle Conference, which was formed in August 1988. Both Murray and Gladys were instrumental in guiding the formation of the conference and its development in its early years. They provided wisdom and strength when there were many questions and fears about the Aboriginal community working in this way in the church. There were also many fears within the circle about honouring and respecting Aboriginal traditional values and teachings.

The members of the All Native Circle Conference had been given a sacred bundle to carry to all their meetings, and were instructed to set that sacred bundle in the centre of those meetings. The bundle contained the Bible, the cross, sweetgrass, tobacco, ashes from the sacred fire, a rock, the talking stick, and the sacred pipe. Placing it in the centre reminded everyone of the sacred path on which they must walk: always honouring and respecting both the traditional Aboriginal ways and the sacred Christian teachings.

Murray, Gladys (as leading Elders), and I (as speaker of the conference) met many congregations, from Alberta through to Quebec. We explained how belonging to the All Native Circle Conference would enhance our involvement and give us a greater say in the workings of the whole church. Not everyone was convinced that church and traditional Native spirituality belonged together, and their objections tested our faithfulness to the teachings of respect and honour.

Murray remembered times when we spent hours being grilled with questions and listening to long compassionate statements by members of the various congregations. Like St. Paul, we occasionally wondered whether we would be stoned before the meeting was over! But then as the meeting ended, we were honoured with gifts and thanks for coming to share with them. This is the Aboriginal way: being honest and open with each other, but always remembering that we are brothers and sisters, and always remembering how to honour guests.

The teachings Murray had received in his early life gave him the wisdom and strength to support all of those who were in the circle. He helped us to continue to keep the sacred bundle at the centre and to honour both Native and Christian ways of walking in the world. He also reminded us, as he had become aware in his own journey, that there were many traditional ways expressed in the different nations of Aboriginal people in North America.

Murray and Gladys and I also spent many hours working with the General Council, the ten conferences, and many presbyteries of the United Church, helping them to understand the gifts of the Aboriginal people. Murray's humour helped in many difficult moments. He and Gladys were instrumental in forming the Elders Council, which advises the United Church General Conference on Native affairs. Murray and Gladys always listened carefully and patiently, and responded quietly and gently after much time and consideration. They would share a story and make us laugh.

Having served on a variety of church committees and organizations, Murray responded to a call in the early 1990s to enter into ministry with his people. In 1998 at the age of seventy-seven, he graduated from the Francis Sandy Theological Centre. He is currently lay pastoral minister at the Alderville pastoral charge, where he has served since 1995.

Traditional way and Christian way

Murray's parents were Christian, and they were open-minded to those who had a different way. His mother had a more challenging time with this. Her father, a Welsh Orangeman, had strongly held views about the Protestant religion.

Traditional ways were not practised on the reserve when he was growing up. There were people around who had special powers, but they did not tell anyone what they were doing. Even today, many of the people in Curve Lake will not go near places of ceremony or sweat lodges, and some regard such things as the devil's work.

Murray grew up believing that Native ways were inferior, but when he was about forty, things changed for him.

> About this time some traditional people from Six Nations came and shared about the Long House Religion. That was the time we had our first pow wow. They did a lot of their traditional dance wearing traditional dress. From that time on, people got very interested in being Native. Before that, if a guy went away from home, he would never say that he was an Indian. He was too embarrassed. He would say that he was Mexican or Spanish, anything else but an Indian. After that time, people began to become proud of their heritage. You saw signs like "Indian and Proud" and things like that.

Although their new-found pride led people to make traditional dress and do more bead work, those who held with the traditional spirituality still did not come forward and celebrate openly. Then in the mid 1970s, Trent University set up a Native studies course. And some people moved to an alternative Native community that followed the traditional way of the Mediwiwin Lodge, the sacred society of the Ojibway people. One of these people, Paul Beaujois, came back and now teaches at Trent. He set up a traditional lodge on a local farm. They provided opportunities for fasting and sweats, and they also had a teaching lodge, but they stayed for only a couple of years.

It was through his sons that Murray became more aware of his heritage. His son Wes went on a fast with the Mediwiwin people, and after the fast he was supposed to have his mother bathe him in cedar water.

> He was coming out of the fast as a new person. We had new clothes for him. He was washed clean. I took Cobe up there, and she performed the ceremony. She had no problem with that, for she was raised with the tradition of respect, as we all were.

In the early 1980s, Murray took part in his first sweat lodge along with Stan McKay, Alf Dumont, and others at the Five Oaks Christian Training Centre. It felt good.

In the late 1970s, Cobe became interested in the Mormon way. Murray supported her in her journey through the baptism and the different levels of teaching. When their daughter Althea was going to Salt Lake City to get her endowment from the church (endowment is similar to confirmation), Murray and Cobe went to support her, and Cobe was delighted to have a chance to see the temple.

For Murray Whetung, there is no conflict between the Christian way and the traditional way of his own people.

> Jim Dumont used to say, "If you tell your story in a good way then I will honour that story."
>
> I see ministry as the opportunity God has given me to share the journey of life with others, to help them experience God's presence and love, and recognize how valuable they are in God's sight. I understand my call to ministry as a chance to use the gifts and skills God has given me to assist others and to share my faith.

For me, God is life itself. He has been good to me and is part of each moment of the day. I see God in the little aspects of life: in the gentle breeze, in the warmth of sunshine, in the strength of the storm, in the quietness of my heart. It does not seem to matter where I am; I see God in that place.

Arthur Ayoungman

as remembered by his family

*Respect others,
be understanding, share,
and if people are angry
or are unkind, pray for them.*

How does one write about someone who lived a humble life and never considered himself to be above others? It was the way Arthur Ayoungman lived his life every day that people remember.

Arthur was born on 7 August 1919 at the Blackfoot Indian Hospital in what is now called the Siksika Nation. He was born a member of the Sayiiks clan, "the Aggressive People." The Bow River runs through the west end of the Siksika nation, where the land has rich top soil for farming and ranching. The family farm is located a mile north of the Bow River and approximately forty miles east of Calgary.

His mother, *Mii-sins-ki-aa-ki*, Rosie Yellow Fly, was orphaned at about three years old and was taken into the household of Canon Stockten and his wife. As a result, she learned to speak fluent English, and she was among the first members of the nation to attend Old Sun Anglican Residential School. She was an avid reader, gardener, and homemaker. Her grandchildren recollect how she would set aside time each morning to read the Bible and to meditate. She was proud to participate in cultural events and was known as a talented bead worker. All her children proudly wore the Siksika traditional clothing that she made for them for special cultural functions.

His father, *Maa-ni-ka-pi*, Anthony Ayoungman, who was about nineteen years older than Rosie, did not attend school and never learned to speak English. He was a traditional Siksika gentleman. He was an extremely devoted, kind, generous, patient, and loving father and husband. Both parents were exceptionally hard working, but they always had time for their children.

Naming ceremonies

Names are important in Siksika culture. They orally preserve the memory of personal or community events. A person usually has several names during a lifetime, and childhood names normally describe physical characteristics. An individual is given a new name for different reasons, the most common being an achievement, which is also honoured in a ceremony. Sometimes a person is given the name of an older relative in order to carry on the name. Sometimes an individual gives his or her own name to someone else as a sign of honouring them.

Arthur was given several names. His childhood nickname was *Ootskapini* — "blue eyes." Another name was *Kayihtsipimuhkitopi* — "rider of painted horse" — a name he later passed on to his grandson Kent. A relative from Montana also passed his name on to Arthur: *Iitssaapaoyosoop* — "cooking when company comes." *Onnistaiksi'ksinam* — "white calf" — his maternal grandfather's name was also given to him.

His latest adult name, *Maistoitsikin* — crowshoe — was given to him by Ben Calfrobe when he acquired the Chief Crowfoot Teepee design at the last Siksika Sundance. This new name was his father's and his great-grandfather's, and it had great meaning for Arthur since his great-grandfather had become his spiritual mentor.

Schooling

As was apparently quite common at that time, a Roman Catholic priest baptized Arthur shortly after his birth. However, since his parents had ties with the Anglican Church, he was baptized also as an Anglican, and when he was old enough, he attended the Old Sun Anglican Residential School located one mile south of Gleichen.

After the school burned in 1927, he went to day school at a church at the west end of the Siksika Nation. But when construction of the new school was completed in 1931, Arthur was once again back in the residential school in the building that currently houses the Old Sun Community College. The students were undernourished. They considered themselves lucky to be assigned to kitchen duties or garbage disposal duties so that they could feast on the leftovers from the staff dining room. All students at the time entered the residential school not speaking a word of English, yet there were punishments for speaking the Siksika language. Amazingly, Arthur was not bitter when he spoke of the past; instead, he shared these stories in a humorous light.

Younger years

In telling stories of his youth, Arthur spoke mostly of his participation in various sporting events. He participated in hockey and was known for being an outstanding goalie. He remembered all the championship games that his team played in. He still played in old-timers hockey games to the age of sixty.

He was active in the sport of rodeo, first as a contestant (steer riding, calf roping, and chuckwagon outrider) and later as a rodeo producer. His love of rodeo was not about money but about the opportunity to participate and excel. He shared many humorous stories about his experiences. Once, when he had just completed his ride and the adrenalin was still pumping, a comrade who had got cold feet asked Arthur to ride in his place. Arthur quickly changed his shirt and got on the bronc. He won the event, but the so-called friend eagerly collected his trophy and prize money. The only thing Arthur got was the enjoyment of riding and some change for coffee. Another friend once asked him to help him out at a chuckwagon meet in a nearby small town. Arthur agreed because he loved being an outrider in these races. They won the event, but his friend once again got the trophy and the prize money.

Later, during his working life, Arthur and his brothers built their own rodeo grounds and held many successful rodeos. Cowboys from the surrounding towns and reserves entered the rodeos and many Canadian champion contestants had their start there. The success of the rodeos was achieved through the hard work and cooperation of the family.

Family life

At the age of twenty, Arthur and Nora (*Iinaksistsiksiina*) Waterchief were married according to the Siksika tradition. Since at the time only a few families still followed this tradition, they were highly honoured by their extended families to be married this way. When her parents first announced that Nora was going to be *Ahkisskowa* ("sent home"), all the Waterchief extended family and *Iiksissakaoyi* ("meat eaters") clan members brought gifts in the form of blankets, fabrics, and moccasins. Eventually Nora, the gifts, and several horses were delivered to the Ayoungman household. Nora speaks of how one room was full of these gifts and her new mother-in-law invited relatives and *Sayiiks* clan members to come for gifts and welcome the new daughter-in-law. A few days later on 22 October 1939, the couple were married in the Anglican Church. The Ayoungman extended family also accumulated reciprocal gifts that were delivered to the Waterchief household.

Nora's father, *Otsiimiyohkitopi* ("sorrel horse rider"), William Waterchief, was a farmer and belonged to spiritual societies. Her mother, *Niitsiini'ki*, Mary, was born in a teepee camp by the Bow River, in Southern Alberta in 1883, seven years after the making of Treaty 7 between the Blackfoot leadership and the Crown. She did not attend the Anglican residential school and never learned English. She lived a very traditional way of life in the rich Siksika culture. She became a medicine woman and eventually a holy woman of the Siksika Annual Sun Dance. Her role as a medicine woman revolved around healing illnesses of the day. She was a "mother" to the entire nation.

Arthur and Nora lived with his parents on the family farm and ranch on the west end of the reserve. Eventually, they all moved to Ksissapohts along the Bow River valley, now called Northcamp, to live with Rosie's uncle when his wife died. All Westend families moved to log homes at Northcamp in the winter because the dirt roads were impassable. In the summer all would return to their Westend farms.

Arthur and Nora had ten children who in turn bore thirty-six grandchilden and thirty-two great-grandchildren. Years later when their children attended Calgary high schools, they drove to Calgary and picked them up every weekend. His children recollect that Arthur never just walked down a street; he always met people he knew and would stop to visit. It appeared that everyone knew him as a friend.

Ranching and other work

Arthur's parents were successful ranchers who owned several hundred horses and cattle. At a very young age his father put him on a saddle, and from then on he helped herd the horses to the river for their morning and evening drink of water. Being the eldest child, Arthur was taken out of school after he finished Grade 7, so that he could help out on the farm and ranch.

As a rancher, he always had a large herd of cattle, and he lost livestock now and then. Horses and cattle were stolen, and most of the time he knew who the culprits were. One of them loaded some of the steers onto a truck, thinking that Arthur would never miss them. But Arthur knew his stock, and he knew they had been stolen. The family couldn't understand why he never pressed charges, but he later explained, " I always figured they must have needed the money more than I did; there must have been something they really needed." His family knew that he prayed for the thieves.

When he butchered, he shared the meat with many. Because there was no electricity at Siksika, he used to have the meat stored in a freezer locker in town. Every time he went to the locker, he got meat not only for his own home but for other households as well. He had grown up in an era when the clan looked out for each other, just as it had in the old days when a hunter returning from the hunt shared what he had taken.

His children used to think that if he wouldn't give so much away, he would be a rich man. Yet he was a rich man in a very different way. He lived to help others; material wealth was not important to him. What you had was to be shared. That's why you had it.

Arthur was known for his hard work and for being a good provider for his family. He enjoyed working; it kept him fit and well. Ranching wasn't his only work. He started a trucking business that involved hauling coal both on and off reserve, and also hauling grain and livestock. But this business, like the ranching, wasn't just about making money. Often he hauled teepees and poles for others, so that they could enjoy participating in cultural events.

Arthur drove school buses for many years. His former students recollect that he was one of the best drivers ever. They were awed that a band councillor would actually drive a bus, an example of Arthur's humility. He never yelled at them. If they got out of hand, he would pull over and start singing. In no time they would all be quiet; he would chuckle and say, "This is how I like to drive the bus — in peace and quiet." Arthur encouraged Nora to get the license required for operating a bus, so that she could take over when he was in council meetings. She also became a well-loved driver. They both prayed every morning for the children to have a safe and good day. She offered words of encouragement to students and even gave attendance awards.

Public life

Arthur was active in the Siksika community. When he was twenty-four, two different hereditary lifetime chiefs considered passing their chieftanships to him because they recognized how deeply he cared for his Siksika people. An older clan relative advised him to wait for the time when he would be ready. Eventually he served for twenty-four years on the band council under the elected system. During this time in politics he served on many community committees and took the time to visit with people and to help out those in need.

He was a mediator when disagreements arose. He reminded people that it was best not to dwell on the negative and on what is over and done with. When some councillors took their roles too lightly, he reminded them to get back on task and focus on the people they were serving.

He was initiated into the Prairie Chicken Society, of which he was a leader for several years. When he likewise initiated a younger member, he became a mentor/grandfather to the Society.

He used to host drumming sessions in the evenings, when singers and drummers came to rehearse or to make new songs. Youngsters who came into his home were usually greeted with a song. Their faces would light up, and they would begin to nod their heads and move their bodies in time with his beat. These young people knew they were welcome. At a powwow Arthur often was one of the first people to dance.

Arthur was the owner of two teepees. Siksika painted teepees are considered sacred, and it is a privilege to own one. Each comes with a song and a story. His mother passed on the deer design to him. The Chief Crowfoot design was transferred to him in a ceremony at the last complete traditional Sundance of the Siksika. (Chief Crowfoot was a key figure in the making of Treaty 7 in 1877.) The late Joe Crowfoot, descendent and previous design owner, explained that Arthur was always good to him, and he knew he could always rely on him for any kind of assistance. Furthermore he knew that Arthur would proudly display the teepee to the world, and would treat it with respect. Arthur's older sister, Mildred, advised that the proper transfer ceremony be conducted, so that the public would never question Arthur's ownership of the design.

When his father, Anthony, was transferring *Iihkitopaasi* (the medicine bundle) to Joe Cat Face, Arthur gave his best race horse, Silent Boy, to his father to use in the transfer ceremony. In the ceremony this particular bundle is carried on a horse to the person assuming ownership of the sacred object; the horse used is given away as well. Arthur wanted his father to give away the best that they had, a strong example that possessions were secondary to generosity and respect for tradition.

Not only was Arthur supportive of local community events, but he was proud to share his Siksika heritage with other people. From infancy he continuously participated in the Calgary Stampede and was a teepee owner at the Indian Village for a long time. Over the years he represented the Stampede, Calgary, and western Canada at different national and international events; for example, he was proud to ride in the 1988 Winter Olympic opening ceremonies in Calgary. When Prince Charles visited Siksika in 1977 to commemorate the one hundred years since the making of Treaty 7, the Crowfoot teepee that Arthur now owned was the lunch venue for the dignitaries.

Arthur's Christian life

Arthur went regularly to the Anglican church with his parents. When he was old enough, he attended the Old Sun Anglican Residential School. While there he served as an altar boy.

Both Arthur and Nora devoted a lot of time to the church. They served on the vestry for many years and supported the church financially through their fund raising efforts. The church used to be at the Old Sun Residential School, but when the school was closed, a new facility had to be found. Constructing a new church was too costly, but fortunately the vestry found an unused church in the Bowness area of Calgary, and arrangements were made to move the building.

In the 1960s, the parents of the reserve's Westend community wanted Sunday school for their children. The parents organized themselves and took different age groups to teach in their homes. A schedule was drawn up, and parents took turns transporting the children.

Arthur became a lay reader and a warden of the church. He attended many workshops, retreats, and conferences. A one-week session at the Cook Christian Training School in Phoenix, Arizona, was important for him.

One of the priests who served on the reserve, the Rev. Donovan Brown, encouraged Arthur to go into the ministry. After a period of training, he was ordained into the diaconate on Easter Sunday 1978, and a year later to the priesthood by Bishop Morse Goodman at the Cathedral Church of the Redeemer in Calgary. He was the first Native to be ordained priest in Alberta. Later that year, when the Rev. Donovan Brown was transferred to another parish, Arthur was given full-time responsibility for the parish of St. John the Divine. He remained there until his retirement. He was happy to be a priest. From the start he did not want any pay for his new position because it was an opportunity to make a total commitment to serve the Lord. However, as he grew older and his other sources of income decreased, he finally accepted a token wage.

His dream was to see at least five Native people ordained in the diocese of Calgary, and he witnessed part of his dream come true with the ordinations of Margaret Waterchief, Mervin Wolfleg, and Sid Black into the priesthood.

As a priest he had a negative experience with the church, almost grave enough to have driven him away. The event so angered one of his daughters that she said, "Mom and Dad have devoted their lives to the church, never missing church on Sunday and volunteering for everything. Now they're being treated so disrespectfully — I'm never going to set foot in that church again." But Arthur, in his very gentle way, explained that people who work for the church are only human and have their own feelings and opinions. "There is a power," he said, "far greater than we are that is infinitely good," and he could never judge the Creator's intent through the actions of people.

Around Arthur it was not possible to be negative. His devout respect for centuries-old Siksika spiritual practices, and at the same time for Christianity, exemplified his deep faith. For him there was no clash between the two.

His basic teachings are etched in the minds of those who were close to him: respect others, be kind and understanding, always share, and if people are angry or are unkind toward you, pray for them.

Burton Jacobs

adapted from a presentation
made at the University of Windsor

Revolution on the reserve:

Exit the Indian agent, enter self-government

I believe in self-government for Native people. In the two hundred and some odd years in which Native people have been under White rule, they have not made any significant advancement. Even today, in spite of the millions of dollars that are being spent annually on their health, welfare, education, and material development, the results are very disappointing. Why is this?

One notable contributing factor is the agency system. In this faulty structure the entire management of the reserve was placed under the supervision of the Indian agent. He was the welfare officer, truant officer, druggist, social worker, taxi-driver, policeman, and judge. By virtue of the Indian Act, all administrative matters relating to an Indian reserve were under the direct control of the Indian agent. You could name anything you want — the management of roads, bridges, schools, housing, welfare, leasing of land, sale of timber, policing, and many others — these were under the direct control of the Indian agent. And although there was a chief and council somewhere, they had little or no significance as a ruling body.

If you wanted to speak to the council, it was always the agent who came forward and demanded to know what you wanted. The chief and council were virtually powerless because the agent had systematic control of the council. He attended every council meeting, and he insisted that no council meeting was official unless he was present. He generally came into the council meeting with a list of items that he wanted the council to pass, and the council generally passed them without question or without any argument. If a councillor expressed a point of view that was unpopular with the agent, the agent would intrude and argue the point, and he generally ended the argument by saying that he would not recommend it.

The last point is worth noting because that was the key to the agent's success. The influence of the agent was actually twofold: he exerted his influence in the council with his recommendations, and he exerted his influence on the resolutions that were submitted to Ottawa, by pointing out which resolutions should be approved and which resolutions should not be approved. Invariably, the resolutions were approved or disapproved in Ottawa according to the agent's recommendations.

The many duties that the Indian agent performed could have been delegated to the Native people, but this was not done. As a result of the failure to provide an opportunity to Native people to take part in the administration of the reserves, they lost valuable and practical experience in business and politics. Not only that; they did not acquire the interest, pride, and morale that are so necessary in any race of people engaged in a struggle. This lack of involvement, without a doubt, has brought about the defeatist attitude and sense of frustration so common in Native people today.

In my personal life, I have found that if you want something done, you have got to do it yourself. This rule also applies when you are dealing with governments; you have got to go after them. The Indian Affairs Branch is not going to do it for you. The fact that you couldn't depend on the Indian agent to transact business to your satisfaction was proven many times on my reserve. For instance, on two or three different occasions the Walpole Island Reserve Council requested that the Indian agent try to get a bridge constructed, but it was not until the Walpole Council was on a self-governing basis that the dream for a bridge began to materialize.

When I became chief in 1960, I was determined to make a change, although I had no clear idea at the time what approach I should take. I knew I had to have the council behind me, but when I first took a poll, only a third were in favour. I was willing to wait until another election came — or even two elections — before I made any moves. I knew that sometime a strong council would emerge with the same views that I had.

In the meantime, I decided to carry around a petition from door to door, to try and solicit support for my cause. This was a very slow and difficult process. I had no problem with those people who made frequent contacts with the agent, because they knew what it was like to deal with him. But I had problems with older people and those who did not make frequent contacts with the agent. They were afraid of change.

One day, after I had been at work for about a year soliciting support, I was surprised to see the Indian agent at my door. He said, "I understand that you are trying to get rid of me. Perhaps we should talk about this." So I took him under the shade of a thorn tree by the river, and we sat down on a bench. He said that I was creating a disturbance and stirring up the people. When the agent left, I thought to myself that this was the beginning of a long drawn-out battle.

The next episode may be coincidental, but I began to receive a lot of attention from the police. They stopped my car a number of times and made a thorough search. They looked into the glove compartment and searched the inside of the car and the trunk. They didn't say what they were looking for, and I didn't ask them, but I suspected that they had some affinity with the Indian agent, and that they were trying to force me to stop what I was doing.

It appeared now that the agent was intensifying his campaign. He used any excuse to attack me and some of my councillors who he thought were my supporters. This had the effect of stirring up a hornet's nest. One councillor was very annoyed. He made a lot of noise when his boy was sent to reform school. I took advantage of the hostile climate that existed to solidify my position.

We began to have a series of private or secret meetings, changing our location each time so that no one could interfere. The last big meeting that we had planned took place in an old abandoned school on the main road. There we composed our resolution to evict the agent. The question still remained: Who was going to present the resolution in council? This would be difficult with the agent sitting and staring at us. When Councillor Brigham introduced the eviction motion to the council, it was voted upon and carried by a clear majority. The motion was like a bomb that exploded on the floor and knocked the wind out of those that were struck by it. The agent and two councillors never said one word during the entire meeting.

Even before the smoke cleared, another enemy appeared on the scene. This was in the form of a citizens' committee that was organized for the express purpose of fighting the council. They invaded our council meeting in a large force, and they sat there, whispering, giggling, and sometimes interjecting comments during the course of the council proceedings. The committee was composed of Indian people who were close to the Indian agent and three employees of the council. They were present at every council meeting, and although they did not create any great problem, the real danger was the possibility that they could grow in numbers.

One time, after a council meeting, one or two of the group came up to me and told me that I should call a public meeting to explain why the council had dismissed the Indian agent. I told them that I would be glad to do that, and that I would post notices up to inform the public. At the meeting I gave a talk; then I gave an opportunity to the citizens' committee to say whatever they wanted to say. Surprisingly, no one wanted to say anything. Afterwards, a lot of the people came forward to shake my hand and to pat me on the back. I felt very good.

The citizens' committee's unsuccessful attempt to win public support did not stop them in their work. They went to Ottawa to petition the minister to remove the chief and councillors from office. We decided to follow them to Ottawa and present our side of the story to the minister. I asked the agent to make an appointment for the council to see the minister. The following morning he said he had forgotten. Knowing that we could not depend on the agent we boarded a train in Chatham and left for Ottawa.

We went straight to the Indian Affairs office. The receptionist said the director was too busy to see us. We called our Member of Parliament, who said that he would call the director and that, if he still refused to see us, he would go right over and talk to him.

By this time, the receptionist told us that we could go into the boardroom to have a meeting with the director. At the meeting, we told the director what we wanted — we wanted the Indian agent removed. The director was stubborn. Then Councillor Simpson Brigham spoke up and said, "If you can't grant us our request, we're going to resign and call a press conference." The director got a little nervous and said, "You can't do that. We'll adjourn this meeting and still continue the dialogue later on."

During the next nine months, the rivalry between the council, the agent, and the citizens' committee went on as usual. The committee demanded an audit of our bookkeeping, but the audit showed that our books were in good order. The next move the council made was to dismiss three employees who were members of the citizens' committee. When the motion was introduced, I think the mover got kind of carried away. The motion called for the dismissal of all council employees with the exception of the secretary.

I think the move we took stimulated some activity on the part of the Department of Indian Affairs because the next day I had a call from the Toronto district office saying, "Bring your council down to my office for a two-day meeting. We'll try and grant you self-government on a trial basis for one year." With some difficulty we came up with terms that were satisfactory to both parties.

After about a year, Indian Affairs made an assessment of our operation, and they were very satisfied. They said self-government was a success, and they started to promote it all across Canada. We had visitors from every province in the country. The seven chiefs from the maritime provinces presented me with a talking stick.

In the space of five years after we went under self-government, we started and completed development programs that cost well in excess of $2.75 million. We built a bridge that cost over $1 million. We constructed a large school that cost over $1 million. And we built the first day-care centre on an Indian reserve in Canada. That's something we are proud of.

Also, since the Indian Affairs Branch has moved off our reserve, the employment situation has improved a great deal. It used to be that when any repair work was required in our five schools, the nursing station, the RCMP barracks, or other buildings under the agent's control, the agent used to call in outside help. Now all the repair work is done by our people.

Another improvement I have noticed under our self-rule is communication. Many of our people feel that they are now better informed concerning reserve business. They feel free to come into the administration office to discuss business problems, and they often do this in their own language. There is far more co-operation now between our people and the office staff than there ever was before. Formerly, the agent's office was virtually a battleground. This is understandable because of a long history of broken treaties, bad land deals, and poor relations that existed between the Indian and the white man.

I have looked at the Indian problem closely for a long,

long time. I have now come to the conclusion that if ever the Native people want to catch up to modern society, one of the most important steps they must take is to adopt the system of self-rule.

Stanley McKay

with Joyce Clouston Carlson

*Growing Up in Family and Community
the Traditional Way*

Fisher River

When Stanley McKay was born in 1911 at the Fisher River First Nation in central Manitoba, the community was firmly rooted in Cree traditions and accessible to the outside world only by a dirt road in good weather.

Fisher River is named after the fisher, a beautiful animal of the marten family. It flows through central Manitoba and empties into Fisher Bay with access to the vast open waters of Lake Winnipeg, the eleventh largest inland freshwater lake in the world. Many First Nations communities have lived along the shoreline for centuries.

When the Canadian government introduced compulsory schooling for all children, Native people had to choose between leaving their children in residential schools ten months of the year while they continued with their traditional lifestyle, or settling in a village with a school. To keep their families together, some people from Norway House, a community on the northernmost shore, decided to move to Fisher River. A permanent village was possible there because the surrounding lands were suitable for farming, gardening, and raising cattle to supplement their hunting and trapping.

As a child, Stanley remained with his mother year round in the village while his father and other community members continued to trap fisher, muskrat, and beaver along the river banks and into the bush. They fished in the shallow waters of Fisher Bay and had access to Lake Winnipeg. The wetlands provided pasture for cattle and horses, and fields for growing hay. The homes stretched along the banks of the river. There were hardly any fences. The cattle lived along the river, staying in the shade of elm and spruce that reached over the river on both sides. Wild fruit — saskatoons, plums, pin cherries, raspberries, strawberries, and cranberries — grew in abundance, and most families tended large gardens. Wood for heating and cooking was available through harvesting deadfall on surrounding Crown lands.

Drinking water from springs along the river was fresh and always clean.

Birth and adoption

In traditional Aboriginal society, every child is honoured as a gift of the Creator. But when Stanley was born out of wedlock, his mother, Harriet Hamilton, was in a difficult situation. The Indian Act stipulated that if the father of a child born on the reserve was from outside the community, the child could not benefit from full treaty rights. A father from the community had to be "named" in order for the child to be considered Aboriginal. The benefits included receiving five dollars per year, a large amount of money in those days, as well as other aids to assist in fishing and farming. More important, when the child grew up, he would have the option of always staying in the community if he chose.

> One day after church my mother placed me in the arms of my aunt because she had a chance for some work; she was going to "cook" in a fish camp. My mother needed the freedom to pursue jobs wherever they were. My uncle and aunt adopted me.

There were no orphans without homes in Aboriginal societies. There was no government staff, no doctors, nurses, or child care agencies. It was an honour to raise an orphan. Parents felt that the Creator looked after children, so it was considered an honour to be one of those who looked after a child without a home.

When Stanley was placed in the arms of his aunt, his mother's older sister, she and her husband assumed responsibility for him. The chief and council formally recognized Nancy Anderson McKay and her husband Samuel McKay as Stanley's adoptive parents. They were childless when they adopted him, and they also adopted a child of Samuel's brother, whose mother had died.

So Stanley grew up within a family who loved him and in a community with values rooted in ancient Cree tradition.

Stanley always knew who his birth mother was. He slept at her home when she was in the community, and she always brought a little gift for him and for his step-sister when she returned from the fishing season. He never knew for sure who his father was.

The chief and council's formalization of the adoption and the community acceptance of the adoption had been considered sufficient. But years later when he was applying for a birth certificate, Stanley learned that his adoption was not legal under Canadian law and he had to pay a fee of one hundred dollars to legalize the continued use of McKay, the name he had used all his life.

Stanley's adoptive father was often away hunting and trapping. He was a devout man. When he was home, the family listened after supper as he read the Bible and talked about it, and then prayed.

Stanley's father spanked him only once. After church one Sunday, Stanley stayed with his grandfather and didn't want to return home. His father spanked him. "It was a spanking I felt — but I realized later that I deserved it!" His mother never at any time hit him or physically punished him. "She always treated me with respect."

Stanley was especially close to his adoptive mother, a woman skilled in traditional knowledge. She skinned and tanned hides and did beautiful silkwork. In those days the women of Fisher River used silk in decorative work rather than beads. Often the young girls did the embroidery, and the older women sewed the moccasins together. Nancy sewed moccasins skilfully, using beautifully coloured silk thread to outline intricate patterns. She had an old pedal sewing machine and sewed women's dresses as well as men's shirts. She made clothes for her family, or to give away or trade for groceries or sell. In those days, she received one dollar and fifty cents for a pair of moccasins.

Growing up in a traditional First Nations community

When I was a boy, I learned about the world around by observation. Many times, I'd be at the end of the dock looking into the water. On a day when there was no wind, the water didn't stir, and I could see the reflections. From where I was kneeling, the sky ran over and under me, surrounding me completely. When I watched the fish swimming, I had to be very quiet because if I moved, even just a little, they'd go to the bottom. If I stirred or made a noise when a muskrat was building his nest, he'd dive into the water and I wouldn't see him again. I learned patience and silence. Sometimes I'd look up in the sky. I could hear birds before I could see them. They were so high, they were almost invisible on a clear day, soaring round and round, way up.

From the day of birth, we were a part of the adult world. We were spoken to and treated as such. We were taught by the example of our older brothers and sisters, or parents or Elders — all members of the community had a responsibility to guide a child. We were taught to reply when spoken to. The main source of teaching hinged on survival. Because of this, we had to have a great concern for our fellow human beings, a deep reverence for animals, birds and fish, things that crawl, things that grow; and we learned that all things are interconnected.

In our culture, if a girl was being taught how to make new moccasins, she stood by her mother and observed how to make moccasins. Learning by experience has a very strong influence. A child would sooner try to copy what you do than do what you say.

Women were givers of life; their role was to help and nurture their children. Men brought food and provided shelter.

When I was old enough, I was taught to do all kinds of different chores. I had to wash dishes, scrub the floor, clean fish, skin rabbits, pluck the feathers off ducks, help tanning hides. One never ending task was carrying water from the river for drinking and washing. Another was bringing in firewood.

We had to learn to hunt, and to hunt well, in order to feed a family. There was great respect for a good hunter, a good provider. Those unable to provide for themselves were cared for. The only way to exist was to be entirely self-sufficient; one had to be resourceful, skilled, and knowledgeable of the habits of animals and fish to survive and to care for one's family and extended family.

When we hunted, we used all parts of the animals. With a moose, for example, the sinew was used for thread for sewing. The head was skinned, and the cheeks and tongue were used. The brain was used in tanning, the hide was tanned, and the meat was eaten. No part of the animal was left to decay. Even the lower part of the leg was used. The bones were cooked slowly over the coals; then the marrow was removed and eaten. The thick hide of the lower leg was cut away and used on the bottom of hunting moccasins. A cow moose in the calving season was not killed unless there was great need.

When my father and other hunters went out, they always gave some of their meat to others. If, for example, a man in another family was sick, he would never be without. Many times I saw men giving others meat, fish, rabbits. Widows and the elderly were also given meat. A responsibility of a young boy might be to chop wood for those who were elderly or unwell.

The only meat that was "preserved" in our community was pemmican, made from moose meat. We built a small wigwam and smoked the meat until it was dry, then placed it between pieces of dried canvas and pounded it with a stick until it was powdery. We melted moose tallow fat, poured it over the powdered meat, and put it in little bags. Blueberries, chokecherries, and saskatoons were also often added to this mixture. It could be preserved for years.

While some accommodations were made to Canadian society, the community remained economically independent and relatively untouched. The people of Fisher River had evolved their social structure over centuries in one of the harshest climates in the world. Their spirituality was closely connected to the Creator and creation. Life was a delicate balance. Community was central to survival.

> Our community was like a large extended family. We were taught not to knock on a door. If we needed something, we often would go to borrow bannock, tea, or sugar from a neighbour. This wasn't kept track of. Our neighbour would in turn come and borrow something from us when they had a need. We learned that the person most respected was the good hunter who shared the most with others, who provided help to those in need. We shared with all. There wasn't one person with plenty and his neighbour with nothing. And we didn't take more than we needed from the land. We shared until no more was left. We shared everything.

Money meant little. Stanley's family was almost completely self-sufficient, purchasing only a few staple foods such as flour, sugar, and tea.

> They said that you could put money away, and it would grow. I thought that was really interesting and I wanted to try it. I had two quarters, and I hid them. After a few weeks, I went to check on them, and found that they hadn't grown at all. There was nothing more than what I had put there.

Elders: Storytellers and role models

Part of growing up was hearing the stories and legends told by Elders. Before the Canadian Government required that children attend schools,[2] families had camped together in small economic units. The men hunted. The women prepared the food and tanned and cured the hides. The children learned from their parents the knowledge and skills that would guide them throughout their own lives.

Elders had a special role in the care of young children. They carried a great deal of knowledge and wisdom, which they were entrusted to pass on to the next generations.

> At times I would go to an Elder with a gift of matches or a bit of tobacco, and the Elder would sit for hours and tell stories and legends. Sometimes the Elders would make a bow and arrow for us, using "grey willow," a kind of wood that we used for fishing as well because it was very buoyant.
>
> There were so many different kinds of birds. When a young boy had killed his first bird, he would take it to his grandmother or another older woman he wished to honour. She would clean it and prepare it in a special way to celebrate the time that the boy had gained enough skill to bring home his first bird.

Community life had a rhythm. Storytelling on long winter nights was the way of teaching the young. Stories told of the beginning of time, of relationships between men and women and the animal world.

---

2. For more informatin on the impact of education, see Joyce Clouston Carlson, *Dancing the Dream: The First Nations and the Church in Partnership.* Toronto: ABC Publishing, 1995.

A main character of Cree legends was Wisahkechahk, a trick-ster who could communicate with all the animals and birds. The beginning of time is told in this way:

> Many years ago there was a great flood. Wisahkechahk and all the animals were on a raft for a very long time. Different animals were sent out to see if they could reach the bottom of the waters to touch land. None of them could reach the bottom.
>
> Then Wisahkechahk sent a muskrat. The muskrat went down, and when he finally came up, he had a bit of mud in his paws. Wisahkechahk blew on the soil and it started to grow. Finally, there was so much land that it went as far as the eye could see.
>
> Wisahkechahk sent an animal to see if the land was big enough for them. The animal came back and said it was not big enough, he would have to make more. So, Wisahkechahk blew on the soil again. Then he sent another animal, and it too came back and said he would have to make more. Again he blew on the soil.
>
> Finally Wisahkechahk sent an animal who said that he had gone as far as he could and still he could not see how far the land went, and so it was big enough.

Storytellers were great orators, trained to remember the smallest details of stories. Because of the responsibility of holding culture and tradition in their memories, storytellers were greatly re-spected. Stories had important lessons for children, such as be-ing on time.

> The animals got together and had a meeting. They said to each other, "We have to do something. The winters are very cold here, and our coats are not warm enough for the winter. Maybe we should ask Wisahkechahk to help us."

So, Wisahkechahk came along and said, "Okay, I'll make warmer coats for you, and I'll let you know when I have them ready so that you can come and get them." One of the things he did was to change some of the coats of the animals for winter. For example, the rabbit's summer coat was brown, but for winter he made a white coat for him. The same was true of the weasel. All these animals got different coats.

The moose was on his way to get his coat too. While crossing a pond, he saw some plants he especially enjoyed, so he just had to stop and eat. He didn't realize that time was going by until suddenly he noticed it was getting late. He jumped up and went to Wisahkechahk to get his coat.

Wisahkechahk looked up at him and said, "I'm sorry, there's only one coat left that's a winter coat. I can't do any more for you now. I don't have any more time to work on anything else for you, and that's the one that is left. You'll have to take it." The coat was too big and hung loose, but the moose had no choice. That's why the moose has a coat that hangs loose and flaps, especially below the neck.

Stanley has often said that the stories do not translate easily into English. He sometimes hesitates to tell the stories because they can sound crude when translated, while in Cree they are playful.

Traditional spiritual values

The families who came to Fisher River had been converted to Christianity while in Norway House, and they were very serious believers.

As a child I was taught Christianity in the Methodist way — before it was changed to the United Church. The people in my community strongly believed the Christian teachings to respect one's fellow human beings; to respect all Creation; not to abuse other people or Creation; and to keep the Sabbath day. As children we had both Sunday school and church. We went to church as a family and sat as families, children with their parents.

Older people went to church every Sunday. One thing they really believed in was that Sunday was a "day of rest." The only work done on Sunday was what couldn't be done on other days of the week, like looking after the cattle. They cut wood on Saturday. We didn't hunt or shoot on a Sunday.

In addition to church, adults had prayer meetings during the week. Elders were the acknowledged spiritual leaders of the community and held leadership roles at these meetings.

These meetings were similar to modern day prayer meetings. People met in homes on the reserve. Six to eight families would meet on a certain evening in one home and another evening in another home. Families travelled to the nearest meeting; the Aboriginal way was to avoid travelling far from home. Two leaders would take charge of the service. Leaders read the Bible in Cree. Then people would talk about the reading and sing hymns. Leaders encouraged community members to speak or to pray.

Most houses were built of logs and had a kitchen attachment on the side of the main building. This is where children gathered, to listen or sleep while the services were going on.

As children we learned quickly that if we were quiet, we could stay up and listen and be part of the group with the adults. If we were noisy, someone came around and told us we had to go to bed. So we learned to be quiet!

In church we had to be really quiet and still. I remember there used to be a doorkeeper, an Elder who always had a cane in his hand. If two or three of us were making a noise, he'd reach forward and poke us once with his stick to remind us to be quiet. If we still weren't quiet, he'd put a child in a pew by himself or herself. We used to watch for that stick!

They even stopped boys from playing baseball on Sunday. But after some of the boys had been away to residential school, when the chief and council tried to stop them from playing baseball on Sunday, they defied the Elders and continued to play.

This defiance of Elders by children was a glimpse of the many changes the community faced.

Special days

Muk ko say ke si kow: Christmas

At Fisher River we used to celebrate Christmas in a special way. At the beginning of December, a leader would be chosen to supervise the work needed for the feast. That leader picked four or five helpers. They found a large spruce tree in the bush and put it up in the church. One of them would write down the names of all the persons who were to receive presents. Nothing was wrapped. All gifts were spread on the tree and used as decorations. Presents were colourful: knitted socks, mitts, leatherwork embroidered with silk thread, yards of ribbons tied in the middle and hung up. Apples strung together on a string were hung among the gifts on the tree.

After supper the church was packed with people. Carols were sung, a prayer was said, and then the presents were given out. We children sat on the edge of the pew waiting for our names to be called. We didn't wait for the second call; we ran down the aisle to get our present. When all the gifts were given out, we all got some candy donated by the store owner.

Families didn't have trees in their own homes; Christmas was celebrated as a community. On Christmas morning the children gathered together as a group and went from house to house wishing everyone a happy Christmas. People would have home baked cookies or a candy which they passed out to us children.

We used to have a school concert just before Christmas. Sometimes we put the same concert on for two nights if all the people could not get in the first night. It was a night we looked forward to, especially as young teenagers. It was a night we found ourselves a girlfriend — many times our first girlfriend.

Oche mi ke si kow: New Year

The New Year's feast would be supervised by the same crew. They would choose the largest house and clear away the furniture to set up tables. Food was donated by all.

Children would slide down the river bank or play football (soccer, we used to call it). Our soccer ball was often made from canvas stuffed with moose hair. We called the New Year's Feast *Oche mi ke si kow,* meaning "feasting day" or "kissing day." We did a lot of wishing each other well during the feast. Men kissed the women, and women kissed the men! It was a good day.

The Queen's Birthday

We used to always celebrate Queen Victoria's birthday — the queen who made the treaty with us. We used to have a pie social before the 24th of May to raise money for prizes and treats for the races. We played football or soccer against the team from another First Nation.

Treaty Days

Treaty Days commemorated the signing of the treaties and took place around the end of June. This event usually lasted three days or more. Almost everybody moved to the treaty grounds and stayed in tents. This is when we were given the government treaty money of five dollars — a lot of money in those days. Storekeepers from the nearby town of Hodgson came with goods from their store to sell because they could get cash for their sales.

It took quite a while for the treaty money and goods to be distributed. There was supposed to be a fair distribution of money and items that were important for fishing and farming. Every man had to go and tell how many children were in his family. Everyone, even a newborn child, received five dollars. Some children were adopted. If they had been adopted from a non-treaty family they wouldn't get the treaty money.

We used to get five balls of twine per person — either size 40 fine or size 25. We used size 25 for sewing moccasins and size 40 for knitting fish nets. In those days everyone knitted their own fish nets. We really relied on getting that twine. In spring, we also received seeds: carrots, turnips, and onion seed. We would buy potato seed from the settlers. We used to receive axes as well as hoes, shovels, and forks to work the garden.

At treaty time we also received flour. This was measured with a pot. Families would bring their own pillowcases or bags to fill, and they would get a scoopful for each child in the family.

Also, we were given a little gunpowder and shot (pellets). In those days, we put a little bit of powder in the gun, then tapped it down. Then we would put in a plug of straw and, after that, some shot followed by another plug. This was called a musket; it was an old type of shotgun. Then we stopped doing this, and people began to use guns with cartridges.

Gradually there were no more seeds, gunpowder, or twine. They did continue to give us flour and salt pork. We used the salt pork for many things. It kept a long time. We sometimes boiled it with dried meat, or if it wasn't too fat, we boiled it to slice for sandwiches.

A special treat at treaty time was ice-cream. We used to cut ice for summer use in the winter. We took a large block of ice from the river and hauled it to a shed lined with sawdust as insulation. This we used to keep meat cool — like a refrigerator. Just about every family had an ice house. We cut small blocks of this ice and placed it in a small cabinet with a tin shelf in the house. This worked like a refrigerator. When the ice melted, we cut another small block and placed it in the cabinet. We were able to use the ice from the block all summer to keep the small cabinet cool. During the summer we sometimes also dug a hole four to six feet deep. We lined it with wood, and could store milk, meat, and fish in that as well. It kept foods quite cool.

When I was young, treaty days were really special. Weddings were special as well — everybody was allowed to go. There was never any need for invitations. Elders had a special role in all community events; they were treated with respect and shared stories.

Glimpses of ancient tradition

Dreams were an important part of Aboriginal life. Lots of older people had dreams and were vision seekers. Also we relied on Elders to interpret the dreams of others. I remember this in my childhood, but it wasn't part of the experience of younger people because the older people wouldn't talk about this part of their lives.

I would dream about a young girl with whom I was walking in the bush. I came to recognize this dream as a sign that I would have good luck in whatever I was doing. As I grew older, I didn't respect this dream and bragged about my good luck. The dreams stopped. I asked an Elder about this once, and he said, "This is a gift that you had. But by bragging about it you spoiled it, and the gift was taken from you."

When I was very young, my grandfather told me that as a young man he had once seen a traditional shaking tent ceremony. He had been travelling with a couple of other men and stopped at a settlement. There was a man training to be a shaman who agreed to show them the shaking tent in the evening. There were poles in a circle and over them untanned hide, which we called parchment. The man went into the tent and began drumming and singing, and suddenly there was a bang and the tent began to shake. There was a voice conversing with the man in the tent. It told him that he must not do this for show — and then it asked if there was anything the visitors wanted to know. One of the men asked if a relative in another camp was still alive. The reply was, "This man is getting along well." Some said that the three men travelling were Christian and this might have interfered with the functioning of the shaking tent.

Many times the older people could tell what kind of winter was coming. They seemed to know if a winter was going to be cold from observing the natural world. For example, they watched the moose closely. A moose, before it mated, would rub its horns on willows. If it scraped its horns low on the willow, this meant that there would not be much snow; if the moose scraped its horns high on the willow, this meant the snow would be deep.

Many of the older people knew and still used some of their Aboriginal medicines to treat different illnesses. This began to change with the arrival of the first outside minister.

The minister had a dispensary in his personal living quarters; from this dispensary he gave out medicines. He strongly discouraged the use of Indian medicines. When the people saw the minister coming, they hid all their medicines from him.

In earlier days children always used to go with their grandmothers to find the traditional medicines, and in this way the children would learn about medicines. The problem was that the older people didn't teach the young people because they were so discouraged by the minister. That's why this knowledge didn't carry on to the next generation. I never learned much about the medicines. The one plant that everyone knew about was *wee kas*, or wild ginger. It's a strong medicine for headaches or bad colds. I remember as kids we used to pick it in swamps. It grew everywhere. We cut, washed, and scraped it, and then tied and hung it to dry. Then it was grated into a powder, and we used it to make a hot drink.

Education the Canadian way

With the support of the Methodist Church, the Fisher River community had set up a small day school so that their children could attend the local school up to Grade 8, and thus satisfy the requirement of compulsory schooling established by the Government of Canada.

When we went to school, we all wore homemade clothing. In the spring we wore beef shoes made out of cattle hide. We had no rubbers. Beef shoes were waterproof, but by evening the tops would kind of dry out, so we would have to put water on them before we could take them off.

As a child at school, Stanley began to experience the differences between his culture and the white European culture brought by the school.

Teaching in schools was a kind of teaching irrelevant to our culture; it wasn't related to our survival. The newcomers brought guns, beads, fire water; they talked about high rise buildings, trains. It was not easy to learn anything the teachers tried to teach us because there was no communication. The teachers spoke only English, and we spoke and understood only Cree. Not many people spoke English on the reserve — only the teachers and the storekeeper. Our teacher had big pictures of animals and birds. And every day she picked up a picture of a mallard, asked what it was, and I'd say "tuck." She replied, "No, it's a duck," and every day my reply was "tuck." She was getting more and more frustrated, and I was getting more and more and more confused. In the Cree language we don't voice the "d"; we pronounce it as "t." And we pronounce "b" as "p."

I couldn't understand the nursery story about Jack and Jill going up the hill to fetch a pail of water. I always went down to the river to get my water.

I used to hear teachers say that they enjoyed teaching Aboriginal children. This seemed to be because the children tried so hard to please the teachers. The word "no"' used to get us into difficulty — not only as children but also as adults. We felt that "no" was a negative word and usually made people unhappy — so we said "yes" to please them. Many times that "yes" would bind us to a commitment. If we didn't live up to that commitment, there was much misunderstanding.

We went to school from around eight years to sixteen years. We went home earlier during the shorter days in November and December. We all had to walk — there were no school buses then. When we got home, there were chores to be done to help our families.

Change comes to the family and community

Stanley's adoptive father died of pneumonia in 1927 when he was in his fifties and Stanley was sixteen. Stanley had gone to the New Year's feast, and word came that his father had passed away, leaving him with new responsibilities.

He began to work off the reserve. In the early thirties he went to a nearby town and fished for an Icelander, earning about ten to fifteen dollars a month. He began to learn the Icelandic language. During harvest season, he earned three dollars a day, working from daylight to dark helping farmers. He cut poplar cord wood for white settlers at seventy-five cents a cord. Sometimes he cut two cords a day, beginning in early morning, and cutting and hauling until well after dark. It was very hard work for a teenager. The wood was in four-foot lengths and a cord of wood was a pile eight feet long and four feet high.

Stanley's adoptive mother supported herself and her family after her husband's death by tanning hides and sewing. Stanley often helped his mother with the tanning; and he hauled, cut, and sawed the wood for her, helped with the cattle, cleaned out the barns, and fed and watered the animals daily. He also helped with smoking of goldeye, a popular delicacy from Lake Winnipeg. Stanley's responsibility was to scale, cut off heads and tails, and slit and clean the fish.

Nancy McKay stayed in her own home, gardened, and looked after her own needs until her death in June 1938. When Stanley was first married, she lived just up the river from the young couple. She often shared with them meat and fish that people had brought her, and she made moccasins and knitted mitts for their children. When Stanley returned from hunting and fishing, he shared with his mother as well.

The wisdom and teachings of family and Elders rooted Stanley's childhood in tradition and informed his view of life. With gentle but firm teachings by example — as well as occasional "pokes in the back" by Elders reining in the antics of young boys — and with a great deal of encouragement, Stanley learned what it was to live and share life in community. Through the most extreme and difficult trials, he has turned again and again to these traditional understandings to guide his life.

A community in transition

"Many people still refer to this old life, when there was a dignity in our lives and a feeling of worth in our outlook, when there was an unspoken confidence in the home and a sure knowledge of the path we walked upon.

"Then there came change. People came. More and more people came, and we continued to live much as our ancestors had — not seeing the value of education. Suddenly, we were in the midst of the twentieth century! Our resources were gone, and there was no time to equip ourselves with the tools of this new age. We were adrift in this new age — but not a part of it!

"Suddenly our reserves had changed. They became plots of land upon which we floated in a kind of unreality, ashamed of our culture which was ridiculed, unsure of where we were or where we were going, uncertain of our grip on the present and weak in our hope for the future.

"It seemed to be the suddenness of the thrust into the new age that hurt so much."

[Chief Dan George, excerpted from an unpublished address circulated at a cross-cultural workshop for teachers in the Winnipeg School Division]

Values at stake:
The coming of white culture

When Stanley began to work outside the reserve as a teenager, he had glimpses of other cultures. Also, there were increasing contacts with non-Aboriginal people on the reserve. In this community which had relied on co-operation for survival for centuries, the fierce competition of traders was hilarious.

I remember when I was a teenager, freighters often travelled using teams of horses to haul fish. One of the teams found that a snowplough worked well, and if they used a snowplough to clear the ice, they could carry a much heavier load of fish on the sleigh. This worked well, but then the group with the snowplough noticed that other groups — their competition — came behind them and were able to carry more loads of fish on the cleared path. So they had their last team fill in the trail behind them to ensure that the other freighters wouldn't benefit from the ploughed trail. We used to laugh at that. The reserve was always working together. The fishermen themselves never seemed to benefit from the competition of the companies who sold their fish.

Some of the experiences with traders were not funny at all.

There was a "stopping off place" where traders often went to eat and sleep. Sometimes they had dances and parties there. Freighters would leave their loads outside and go in.

Teenagers didn't have many places to go or things to do. They weren't allowed to go to parties or dances, and so on this night, a few teenagers got into one of the loads on a traveller's cart. They found some jam in it, and each took a two-pound can. The trader called the police, who caught the boys and charged them with theft. As a punishment for being "thieves," these boys were sent to residential school in Brandon. In those days, children who were considered troublemakers could be sent away. The Indian agent or the police could make this decision, and parents had no say.

The residential school experience often proved to be a very severe punishment. Children who attended were immersed in a totally different culture without the support of family and community. They often had extremely difficult experiences. Officials divided the children by age; some went to Birtle, and some went to Brandon. Stanley's friends remained in the schools until they were sixteen.

Stanley was troubled by the description his good friends gave of their experiences at the schools.

The schools had barns with cattle, and the students milked the cows — but the milk and cream were sold, and they gave the children only skim milk. My friend's job at the school was milking the cows. At home he used to have whole milk on his porridge every day, but at the school they had oatmeal with skim milk. One day he found a little bottle small enough to put in his pocket. He filled it with cream, and when he came in for breakfast, he'd sneak out the bottle of cream and share it around for the kids to use it on their porridge. Someone must have told on him. When the school found out, they made him hang the bottle around his neck for a number of days.

It was really embarrassing for him. What I never could understand was why the teachers and staff at the school seemed to shame the children, to make fun of them, and to make them feel bad. Why would a school sell the milk and cream, and not give it to the children? Also, they had a big garden. Why wouldn't they make sure the children were properly fed? And in one of the schools, the staff had their own dining room and a different menu from the children.

They always said that they were teaching children a different culture, but they never seemed to give children opportunities to learn how to make decisions. They were always told what to do; they were just following orders, not learning how to make decisions themselves.

There were other intrusions over which the community had little or no control.

The abuse of the environment by surrounding settlers and fishing companies led to a lack of fish and animals, and thus to a loss of livelihood. Then there was alcohol.

As I grew older, there was quite a bit of brewing of "moose

milk" — home-made beer. Also some settlers in local towns knew how to brew and sold beer to the guys on the reserve. Sometimes people drank too much, and sometimes they would fight against each other. In those days they never fought with weapons; they might get a black eye because they fought with fists. They didn't feel it was right to fight with weapons.

Church, police, and Indian agent

The first outside minister to the community taught on the reserve for two years, and later, after learning Cree, returned again as a minister. There was an unfortunate connection between the mission house, the police, and the Indian agent.

> I never saw the police as a force that would help or protect. The only time the police ever came to the reserve was to pick up one of our friends. Police came out periodically to the reserve, and when they came, the manse was the first place they went. The people saw this happening, and they didn't like it.

As settlers moved closer to the reserve, there were increasing problems with neighbouring communities. Some of their reserve animals simply disappeared. Cattle and animals roamed freely in community pastures and were known within the reserve by their markings. Previously, if disputes arose, the chief and council settled them. Police were never called to settle affairs within the community. The police worked in close collaboration with the Indian agent, and the rules of the Indian agent weren't fair to Aboriginal people.

> The Indian agent controlled everything. If you had a steer and wanted to sell it, you had to go to the Indian agent fifteen miles away for a permit. If Aboriginal people didn't get a

permit, the buyer could be fined for buying the animal! It troubled me that it didn't seem to matter to the Indian agent if we got a fair price; it only mattered that we got a permit. How could we get a fair price? If we wanted to sell, it was because we needed cash — and the buyer knew this. So he offered a very low price, knowing this. The permit system favoured buyers and prevented Aboriginal farmers from having control over our own affairs.

We were taken advantage of in many ways by the rules of the Indian agent, and we had no way of appealing the mistreatment. Once the chief and council were extremely upset over the handling of a matter by the Indian agent and sent a letter to Ottawa with a request for intervention. Ottawa sent the letter back, telling the Indian agent to deal with it; the agent was mad, and the chief and council were in bigger trouble.

Even spiritual life changed. Until the beginning of the thirties, the Elders had led the spiritual life of the community, including the local Methodist church. Stanley, along with many other community members, took great pride in the church. Some of Stanley's woodwork remains in the church today. As a young man, Stanley had an upsetting experience with the a minister.

When I was painting the church hall the minister came by to talk to someone about putting a washroom at the back of the hall. In passing, he made the statement, "All of the people in Fisher River are crazy but me and [an Elder]." As he walked by, I said, "Thanks for calling me crazy." Later he apologized. He seemed to have a lot of compassion for people who were ill, and his Cree was pretty good.

Other churches began to come in, and they were different. They often asked the people who attended for money to "do the work of the church." Our own Elders had never done that.

Marriage and after

Stanley met his wife, Dorothy, at school, and they had opportunities to see each other at the many special community celebrations. Neither had attended residential school. He was twenty and she was seventeen when they were married.

In the early part of their marriage, they continued to live as their families had lived. Stanley built a log house. He hand cut and shaped the logs, chinking them with mortar inside and out, nailing willow branches between the logs to ensure the mortar was firm. He and Dorothy planted trees around the house, and built a barn for animals. Having learned hunting and trapping from his father, Stanley now began to learn commercial fishing by going out on the lake with his father-in-law, Bill Hudson.

One of the hardest experiences of his life was the death of his brother Stephen, five years after Stanley was married. There were fewer and fewer animals around Fisher River. Like many young trappers, Stephen had to go farther and farther to find and trap animals. The east side of the lake was Canadian Shield country, unsuitable for farming but offering rich trapping. In the fall of 1937 Stephen got separated from his trapping companion, and the RCMP found his boat overturned and his body on the path to a trapper's cabin nearby. Lacking warm, dry clothes and matches, he had frozen to death.

> Stephen's body had been wrapped in canvas and buried by the RCMP in a shallow grave. Our mother was concerned because she knew he hadn't had a proper burial. She couldn't rest easy until his body was brought home.

Stanley was one of the four men chosen for the task of bringing the body home — a seven-day trip. After they had found the grave, they had to go to the RCMP station to request permission to dig it up and bring Stephen's body home. The older three men took responsibility for lifting the body from the grave. They told

Stanley not to do the lifting; they strapped the body on a toboggan. They arrived home on a Sunday evening, and the church bells rang out to greet them, as people were entering the church for their evening service. A funeral service was held a few days later at Fisher River United Church. Stephen is buried beside the church. He was thirty-two when he died.

Fishing

Fishing in fall was for pickerel. We had to be really good navigators to use the sixteen- to eighteen-foot skiffs with flat bottoms. Every man had about ten nets. We often camped along the shore. Looking at the stars, we could tell when daybreak was nearing, and we used to boil a kettle of water on an open fire and go out in boats just at daybreak. If it was going to blow or storm, we'd try to be through before the storm arrived.

Winter was the most important season for commercial fishing. When he was first married, Stanley began working like many other men in the community as a hired man for his father-in-law, who bought nets from the company for which he was working. The season began in November and continued to mid-March.

The first year we went winter fishing, the water was still open. We stayed in the camp until it froze and the ice was thick enough to go out on. In the meantime we tied the nets and attached the stones to weight them. Everyone wanted to get the nets set early in winter, so when the men went out on the ice, sometimes the ice would break away from the shore, and people would be stranded out on the ice floes. We sometimes left one man on shore. If the ice cracked, the man on the shore could always manage to row out and rescue the stranded men.

We used long straight poles to set the nets. The poles were about three inches in diameter; we would tie them together so that three poles would make a length of about thirty feet. We pushed them under the ice when it was just forming, and we could see the pole. When we reached about thirty feet, we chopped a hole in the ice, and we kept on pushing the pole until we got to the length of the net. Then we pulled the pole along under the ice the length of the net. We had to remember where the nets were set so that, even when the weather was bad, we could find them. When it was snowing or blowing, we had to shake the snow from the nets as we put them into the water. If there was snow left on the nets, they would float and freeze under the ice.

In later years, two men working in pairs might have as many as thirty to forty nets to look after. Instead of long poles, they set nets under the ice using jiggers.

In early years, after the ice was safe, a horse pulled a canvas caboose out onto the lake to provide some shelter and a place to eat lunch and keep wet mittens. Dog teams were used to haul the fish back to camp, then later horses, and later still, small tractors. Each of the nets had to be lifted every five or six days or the fish would get soft. When nets were lifted, the fish were taken back to the camp area where they were laid out to freeze and then packed in boxes. At the camp they were picked up by the company that had hired and provided nets to the fishermen.

Fresh unfrozen fish brought a higher price to the company. To keep it from freezing, coal oil lanterns were placed at each end of covered boxes lined with cardboard, and the company owner would come every afternoon to pick them up.

Camp was a cabin with bunks, built on the shoreline. They left the cabin every day before daybreak and were out on the lake all day, returning long after dark. They cut wood to take with them to boil water in a kettle. It was difficult to return to the cold cabin and prepare supper. In earlier days, when families camped and fished together, the elderly, and sometimes women and children, would stay at the camp, caring for the fire and cooking, so that when they returned, there would be a hot meal. When Stanley fished, he would sometimes hire a young girl or an older person to stay at the cabin and look after the fire and cook.

In the long winter, they were out on the lake for weeks at a time. Christmas and New Year's were the only breaks in the season. The lake was unpredictable. Even seasoned fishermen could experience difficulties.

> Sometimes the ice would crack. It seemed to crack in the same place each year. In the cold, this crack would open out. In warm weather, it would heave. These cracks were treacherous when we tried to cross the lake with teams of horses.

To keep their hands from freezing while pulling nets from frigid waters, each fisherman would take five or six pairs of Icelandic woollen mittens. When a pair became wet, he placed it in a pocket in his parka. At the end of the day, the mitts were rinsed and hung on racks near the stoves in the fishing cabins. To protect their feet, the men wore moccasin rubbers with felt insoles and two pairs of Icelandic socks.

Summer fishing was about a two-month season. They used gas boats with three or four men to one boat. Commercial fishing in the summer was for whitefish. Whitefish didn't come as far south as the Fisher Bay area, so many from the community travelled to the big basin in the northern part of Lake Winnipeg to fish. Stanley didn't usually participate in spring or summer commercial fishing.

> In spring there weren't many fish. Fishing in this season was pickerel, jackfish, and sauger, a brownish grey fish with a shape similar to pickerel, but smaller. I pulled up nets, hung

them, and put them away. Nets were cotton and linen. They had to be washed and dried properly or they would rot. Much later, about the time when I quit fishing, nylon nets were coming in. I can remember coming home at night in the gas boat, and I could usually see the tree line in the dark. From the trees, one could judge the mouth of the river, and be sure to be in the middle.

A family adjusting to change

With their children still very young, Stanley and Dorothy knew changes were escalating. When Stanley hung up his nets in spring, his work had increased at home.

> When I quit fishing in spring, I began to cut cordwood so that it could cure and be ready for use in fall to heat the homes. When I was young, we had used deadfall, but this was not allowed by the government. As soon as I stopped fishing, my next big job was cutting green wood, hauling it home, and sawing it with a portable saw; it had to be cut into one and one-half- foot lengths to dry, and I had to split it. If I didn't split the wood, it wouldn't be ready to use in the fall for heating. The forest ranger fined anyone hauling wood from lands off the reserve, so trees were left to rot instead of being used. This made no sense at all. As soon as I finished the cordwood, it was time to make hay for the cattle to eat in winter.

Firewood was one of the first resources to go, but there were many, many changes. Farmers off the reserve burned the land to prepare it to be broken and farmed, and dug ditches in the wetlands to drain them quickly in the spring so that they could plant their crops earlier, thereby lengthening their growing season. Increased drainage caused a quick run-off, creating floods in spring and very low water levels later in the season.

The deforestation of lands surrounding the community, together with rapidly changing water levels, destroyed the habitat of water animals. Drainage of the wetlands destroyed waterfowl nesting areas. Hunting and trapping became more and more difficult. Stanley was away from his family for increasingly long periods of time, longer than in previous generations because he had to go farther and farther to hunt.

Stanley and Dorothy supplemented the depleted hunting with cattle and livestock. But drainage of the surrounding area affected their own haylands. After the gardens were planted, Stanley made hay to store for the cattle to eat during the winter. This took most of July and August. They raised chickens and bought one or two piglets in the spring and slaughtered them in the fall. When Stanley was away, Dorothy and the children milked the cows and stored milk in crock jars in the cellar until it had cooled and the cream had risen to the top. They skimmed the cream and churned it to make butter.

> I helped with planting the garden in the spring once the wood had been cut. While I did the haying for the cattle, Dorothy and the children looked after the garden over the summer. They did all the vegetable harvesting themselves as I was always away for fall fishing. We grew all our vegetables to last the whole year, storing potatoes, turnips, and onions in the cellar.

Dorothy preserved fish and moose meat as well as vegetables, jam, and jellies. She invented interesting preserves, mixing wild fruit with vegetables such as squash (sometimes called vegetable marrow) from the garden to make marmalade. She and the children picked the wild fruit in the evenings after her other work was done. She was extremely busy. She made her own bread and cheese. A lot of time was spent in preparing, preserving, cooking, and cleaning. Since there was no plumbing, dishes were washed with water heated in the reservoir at the back of the stove. Elders and community members helped when Stanley was away.

The house was two storeys, with a kitchen added on to the main living and dining area. The cellar was dug under the kitchen and accessed through a trapdoor. The upstairs had three bedrooms; people often stayed with them.

The end of the fishing

Commercial fishing, Stanley's main way of supporting the family, became more and more difficult. The changing water levels altered the spawning grounds of the fish, and increased use of pesticides that drained into Fisher Bay further damaged the fishery. Prices were controlled by the company that bought the fish, and at times fishermen finished the season in debt to the company.

Then in the early fifties, huge company-owned trawlers began fishing on the lake. There were laws stipulating the size of nets that could be used, to ensure that smaller fish would not be taken, but would continue to grow and replenish the stock. These laws applied to both Aboriginal and non-Aboriginal fishermen. Aboriginal fishermen had all their nets and equipment confiscated if they were found using a smaller sized net than was allowable by law. There were no laws, however, governing who fished, where or how they fished, or how many fish could be taken.

The area of Fisher Bay was targeted, and a huge volume of fish was taken. Stanley's son Stan McKay,[3] a teenager at the time, comments on the distress of the community.

> My father often returned from a hard season of fishing with very little. If fishing was poor, prices rose and fishermen were

---

3. Stan McKay, son of Stanley and Dorothy, was ordained a United Church minister in 1971. He was elected Moderator of the United Church of Canada in 1992.

able to pay their expenses. When fishing improved, instead of giving more to the fishermen, the companies moved their prices down.

Fishing was the life of the community. When nets were set across the mouth of Fisher Bay, all of the fishing for the community was depleted. This intrusion into their way of life meant that they had to go farther and farther north for their fishing.

This was before the discussions of Aboriginal rights began. My father wasn't angry. I was much more angry than he was, because I saw the immense greed and aggression in this act of extraction of the fish. This was a crisis in livelihood for the Aboriginal community, in their dignity and hope. It was symbolic of the greed and aggression that eroded the way of life and value system of the community.

There was a significant decline in quality of life there. Until then, people had lived a subsistence lifestyle with some comforts for their hard work. They had a kind of contentment with "what is enough," and they actually felt pity for people who always wanted more.

The government, through the Indian agents, had never been at all pro-active on behalf of Aboriginal people. They didn't do anything to ensure fair prices or fair treatment. In spite of this victimization by government and commercial interests, the people had a capacity to cope, and they had some self-confidence. I believe this was because, in my parents' generation, people had grown up with strength and hope and vision; they had foundational values from their shared life in the community and close connectedness to the environment. Even with the diminishing of life by the Indian agent and the greed of commercial interests, they were able to retain positive life values.

People who haven't had the blessings of these very positive foundational life values become aliens in their own land.

They live with hopelessness and rootlessness. This is now widespread in Aboriginal communities, particularly in urban centres where children have been cut off from the values of grandparents, as their own parents struggle to survive in an urban area separate from their own communities and culture.

What many don't understand about our Elders is the way they were able to withstand the change and retain their integrity through silence. Silence in Aboriginal communities was their way of responding to the devastating changes. Silence is a non-aggressive behaviour, but it doesn't mean giving up; for the Elders it meant an opportunity to be reflective and sort out meanings. But for the next generations, the stories held in silence need to be told so that the children can understand the deep devastation these people endured, why they kept silence, and how it was possible to do so. Theirs was a silence signifying strength.

In 1951 and 1952, a permanent year-round road was built into Fisher River. Stanley stopped fishing and began working as a manager in the local store. The storekeeper, about the same age as Stanley, had a disability resulting from his foot and leg having once been frozen, which made working long hours in the store difficult. Stanley had responsibility for supervising the store, dealing with salesmen, and placing all orders. He even had permission to sign cheques on behalf of the owner. This was during some very difficult years in the community, years when people sometimes couldn't pay their grocery bills — an added stress for Stanley.

Education: Challenge and opportunity

It seemed to me that any progress, any program was just to make the rich richer, and the poor didn't benefit much from it. Aboriginal people especially had little advantage and little education.

We saw the importance of education, and we tried to encourage our children to keep on. It was the only way for them to avoid enforced dependence. We had always been very self-sufficient. We believed our children had to prepare to live in a world that was going to be very different for them. How could they prepare themselves to live outside Fisher River? The only way to do this was through education.

Initially Pat, their oldest, had tried to take Grade 9 by correspondence. But when she had a question, there was no one to ask. Her parents had not gone past Grade 8, and no one else in the community could help either. Reluctantly the decision was made to send her away to school.

For our children to get an education past Grade 8, residential school was the only possibility. When we sent Pat to residential school, it was very hard. We chose Brandon because it was run by the United Church, and we had always been members. We drove her twenty-seven miles to Hodgson. There was a truck there to take her and the other students to Brandon — a cattle truck with rails on the sides. There were benches along the sides, but the children were going a long way on back roads.

Pat at age fifteen had been very excited to go away to school, but the excitement was short lived. She describes her arrival in Brandon:

We were marched into a building. I wanted to turn and run. They took all our clothes. They gave us what they called a uniform. We weren't allowed to have anything personal. They put our heads in coal oil to kill anything we might have. Even though I didn't know the word, I felt prejudice, I felt racism.

Stanley and Dorothy were never happy about the long periods of separation. They knew that the experience had been extremely harsh for Stanley's friend who had attended residential school. They knew that food was often not adequate, and that the children would be lonely.

> What could we do? We had to put up with that if we wanted her to get an education. It was even harder with our second, Doreen. She was very shy and quiet; she was crying and crying and hiding her head in her hands as the truck pulled away.

The year that Doreen left, the parents were so anxious about their girls that they visited after fall fishing.

> We travelled by train all the way to Brandon; the school was three miles from town, so we got a room downtown. We phoned to ask whether we could take them out the following day. They said it was okay, but we had to bring them back by a certain time in the evening. We took a cab to pick them up.
>
> At the school, we rang the bell and a man came to the door. He asked us what we were looking for. I told him we were supposed to be picking up our two girls for the day. He asked us to come in. We went into a kind of a lobby. He told us to sit down. He contacted somebody. We sat there and never spoke to anyone until the girls came out of the door with a lady. She was the matron and she said, "Here they are. We expect them back at seven o'clock." When we took them back that evening, the same thing happened. We went to the door. A man came and opened the door for us. He went in and he contacted somebody. A lady came and whisked them away out of sight. We stood there for a few minutes. Nobody would even talk to us. So we left. They never even talked to us.

The children never complained to their parents at the time. It was only after they were adults that they began to talk about the treatment they received and the depth of their loneliness.

Brandon is now known to have been a particularly difficult school where children were often undernourished. At Pat's initiative they transferred to Birtle, and the school situation improved. Children and staff ate together, and when Stanley and Dorothy visited, they were invited into the school, saw where the children stayed and slept, and talked to staff. However, the separation was still painful in such a close family.

The departure of each additional child to residential school increased the pain. By 1959, four of their five children were living outside the community, either working or studying, and their fifth was ready for high school. Having children who could not participate in family or community life was a total departure from all their cultural understandings. Stanley and Dorothy simply couldn't stand to send their fifth child away to residential school. Both parents wanted to be able to be closer to their children, to provide encouragement to them, as they educated themselves to earn their livelihood in a totally different way than anyone in their family had ever done. So Stanley at the age of forty-eight, and Dorothy at the age of forty-five, decided to leave Fisher River and move to Winnipeg.

A move to the city

Moving to the city

> I saw and felt no differences between myself and others while in Fisher River; I was in the majority there. When I moved to the city, I realized that people saw me as different.
>
> I came from a culture in which I felt a part of everything. In the city I felt a nobody. I was not respected. I was one of a stereotyped group. I was no longer an individual. In order to survive in this competitive society, I had to change my

values. My first concern had to be "me" and my family. No longer could I share what I had with others — because others didn't share with me.

Stanley and Dorothy brought a few belongings to Winnipeg using the storekeeper's truck. They stayed in the small one-bedroom basement apartment where their daughter Pat had been living. Pat had married a man serving in the armed forces, and they were transferred just at the time that Stanley and Dorothy were moving. Ada began school in Grade 10.

Stanley had been encouraged by a government official who assured him that his store experience would put him in a good position to get a job. He promised to help him find one. Dorothy got a job right away at the Indian Métis Friendship Centre, but Stanley couldn't find one. After about a month he called the official to ask for some help in getting a job, and the official took him to Scott Bathgate, a large Winnipeg distributor with two warehouses. Stanley began working there at tasks that were very simple for someone who had managed the store in Fisher River, but at least the owner was friendly.

Soon the family moved into a three-bedroom apartment because family and friends stayed with them from time to time. They were happy to be visited often by their son Stanley who was studying education and staying in a student residence at the Manitoba Normal School in the city. Young Stanley was eventually ordained minister in the United Church in 1971, and in 1992 was elected moderator.

Stanley and Dorothy were increasingly aware that their own experience of alienation and cultural change was shared by many people. Even church was a difficult experience at times.

I felt very uncomfortable when I went to church. The churches were so large, and people were so well dressed in their furs and expensive suits. I was dressed in the parka I wore to work every day. But the worst was I didn't know anyone, and no one spoke to me. I was fortunate while new in the city to know a minister who had spent some time in Fisher River. We attended his little church, Stella Mission, even though it wasn't the closest to where we lived. He was a real support to us.

A new ministry begins

The sixties were a turbulent time. The low fishing stocks and the depletion of game affected many Aboriginal hunters. Their movement to urban areas changed the lives of the First Nations forever, and it changed the face of the city of Winnipeg, which rapidly became the largest urban centre of First Nations population in Canada. Also, increasing numbers of First Nations people were travelling to Winnipeg for medical assistance. They had little money and no place to stay while in the city. The United Church responded to the plight of Aboriginal peoples in the city by proposing an Indian/Métis Reception Lodge.

The first difficulty in this plan was being accepted in the neighbourhood. When the United Church of Canada purchased a building in Winnipeg's north end, the neighbours protested; they didn't want "drunken Indians" living in their neighbourhood. They believed their properties would be devalued, and the streets would not be safe for their children. A doctor with a home in the area led a group of neighbours opposing the project. The matter went to court, and the court ruled that the project could continue. The building was named *Ka pay see wi ka mick*, the Indian and Métis Reception Lodge, and the person approached to be the first manager was Stanley.

Stanley was involved in extensive renovations to the building. They made a suite for Stanley's family on the main floor, and several large rooms on the second floor were rented out to women and children for the nominal fee of seventy-five cents a night per person. The third floor was used as a dormitory for men. The house could accommodate twenty-one people and it was usually full.

> When I first came to the city, I felt that the best thing was for Aboriginal people to integrate. I still feel that way. But we need a "stepping stone," a way to integrate gradually to avoid the culture shock. Some people take very lightly the plight of the Aboriginal person. They say that many people have had it tough, but they have made it, and they wonder why the Indian hasn't.

What most people don't understand is the difficulty of changing from a sharing culture to a culture in which "each looked after his or her own." Stanley describes this difficult transition.

> I remember once a young man who had left his wife and two children on the reserve. There was no employment there, and he wanted to be off welfare. He found himself a job and he did really well. Then he sent for his wife and children, and they established themselves in a little apartment. Many members of his family came to stay, partly because they wanted to find a job and move to the city as well. It was too much for him.
>
> He couldn't support himself, his wife and children, and all of his extended family, on the salary he was making. And his landlord didn't like so many people living in his house. To ask the relatives to leave went against how he believed he should live. So he gave up. He went back to the reserve with his wife and children, and had to go on welfare again. They moved to the city again a few months later, but this time he rented a house out in the suburbs. It was so far out that it was hard for his relatives to travel there. So he was able to live

and support his children and wife, but he didn't have the support of his family, and he had to go against his culture to succeed in this way.

I saw this happening over and over again. This was what made the transition to life in the city so difficult for our people. We almost have to choose between our culture and being able to succeed on the terms of the dominant society.

In addition to dealing with the opposing values of the "dominant society" and the Aboriginal society, Aboriginal people invariably also suffered from discrimination and prejudice.

Prejudice affects people differently. Some become hostile and belligerent. Others say, "What's the use? I might as well be what people say I am." Some manage to survive through it and prove that they are individuals. The most difficult thing to overcome is being part of a stereotyped group. You not only have to prove yourself, you also have to bear the burden of the rest of your group. Discrimination is like a disease. You don't know what it's like until you've experienced it.

I remember two young women who were living in the lodge and had a job in a local sewing factory. They were just out of school. One of the girls was doing her best and going to work every day and on time; the other girl wasn't there every day and was sometimes late. The boss said that the second girl wasn't dependable "because she was Indian."

I tried to convince the first girl not to quit or stop doing her best because if she quit, this would just convince the boss that he was right in what he said about Indians. But the boss kept saying, "These Indians — you just can't depend on them," and eventually she felt so discouraged that she quit.

Many people struggled with these same issues. Stanley and Dorothy did a lot of counselling in their work at the Reception

Lodge. They tried to understand the differences between their own culture and the dominant society. Their children experienced their own share of difficulties in following their dreams. Pat had wanted to be a deaconess in the United Church. Indian Affairs was not prepared to fund education for ministry. They were prepared to fund business administration, and so she pursued that career. Their son Stanley had wanted to take arts and study theology. At that time, Indian Affairs refused to offer ongoing financial support. Stanley went into education and taught several years before returning to university. He paid his way through a degree in Arts by working at construction jobs over the summer. He was ordained and began serving a pastoral charge in 1971.[4] Emily and Doreen both became teachers. The youngest, Ada, was funded by Indian Affairs to become a bookkeeper.

One of the hardest things for people to experience was isolation and separation from family and friends. Stanley and Dorothy got together with others who were experiencing the same culture shock, and supported the Friendship Centre Movement, which had just begun in the late fifties. This movement assisted Aboriginal people to have their own voice and to make the transition to urban life.

---

4. Stan served congregations in Norway House and Fisher River before being named National Coordinator of Native Ministries in 1982. He served as coordinator for five years before leaving to become the Director of the Dr. Jessie Saulteax Resource Centre in 1988.

A family in the city

A home is more
than roof and walls
or lofty curving stairs.
It's love inside
and faith and trust
and softly spoken prayers.[5]

Death and a new beginning

Stanley's wife, Dorothy, died suddenly at the age of forty-eight in 1963. Her sudden death was a devastating blow. One day at lunch she wasn't feeling well. She went to lie down while Stanley cleaned up the dishes. When he went to see how she was doing a few minutes later, she was unconscious. She died the same day. The cause of death was an aneurism, which doctors felt may have been related to viral meningitis, which she had had in Fisher River.

A woman named Verna Crooks had been appointed by the Women's Missionary Society to work in Winnipeg with Native people. Verna was a graduate of the United Church Training School and Dalhousie University, whose theological studies prepared her for a ministry of education, service, and pastoral care. She had arrived in town in 1961, two years after the McKays. New to the city and far from family, she was welcomed and befriended by Dorothy. Over the next three years, Dorothy and Verna became very close friends.

---

5. A poem, embroidered by Stanley's deceased daughter Doreen Lukaszuk, displayed in Stanley's and Verna's family room.

Following Dorothy's death, Stanley continued with his work at the Reception Lodge, on duty twenty-four hours a day, seven days a week. In 1964 the church appointed an assistant to relieve him for three hours a day five days a week. He often used this time to go with First Nations people to social agencies or hospitals, interpreting their needs to officials.

Stanley's and Verna's friendship deepened and grew as they continued to work together. They realized that they wanted to be married, but Stanley was concerned about their difference in age. However,

> When I married Verna, a woman much younger and of a different culture, all five children were very accepting of the marriage. The community as well was very accepting of Verna. They have continued to be very supportive of us.

Their wedding on 1 September 1966 at St. Giles United Church in Winnipeg was attended by about two hundred family and friends. Verna's parents, two brothers, and a sister came from Nova Scotia. Many people came from Fisher River. All Stanley's five children with all their children came as well, including two of his children from the east coast.

Immediately after their marriage Stanley and Verna talked about having children. At this time, with the social problems faced by many Aboriginal families, an unprecedented number of Aboriginal children were in the care of Child and Family Services and in need of permanent placement. Stanley had noticed that young girls, unable to care for their children in the city, often took them home to parents and grandparents on the reserves, as had happened in previous generations. However, now families on reserves were often overwhelmed with responsibilities. So Verna and Stanley adopted two infants: Kevin, a Chipewyan baby from the Sudbury area, and Kirk, a Cree from northern Manitoba.

The experience of raising children in the city was totally

different from raising children in Fisher River. Stanley and Verna felt the pain of watching their children face severe racism both in their schools and in the community.

It was one thing to experience and confront racism as an adult, after having developed very strong self-esteem in the community of his childhood, as Stanley had. It was quite another to see his own children mistreated. Verna was a strong support and ally.

When Kirk and Kevin were three and five years old, young Stanley and his wife, Dot, were in Fisher River and invited the boys to spend a week there. When they came back to the city, they were changed.

> They realized they were part of a community of people who were like them; this made a profound difference to their understanding of themselves, of who they were and where they belonged, even though they were very little. Kevin was in school at the time, and just beginning to experience what it was like being different.

Throughout the boys' school years, Stanley and Verna worked to create a better understanding. They became well known as speakers because they were able to describe the challenges their children faced, as well as their own personal experience as a cross-cultural couple.

> Armed with knowledge and some experience, we went out to share what we had learned. We spoke to service clubs, churches, schools — everywhere. It was a frustrating as well as rewarding experience.

Meanwhile their own learning continued.

> I learned that I could not provide a meal to everyone who needed a meal. I could not provide a bed to all my friends

who needed one. I learned that I had to look after my tomorrow before I could help someone with a need today. Today I hope I have reached more of a balance.

I have been well blessed. But I have used my blessings as I received them. I have not stored the earthly things in a bank. My culture has taught me to live for the present and that, in doing so, my future would be provided for.

Stanley's tendency to live for the present rather than the future has meant some stress in their lives. Summer vacation plans were sometimes difficult to make. It was sometimes extremely difficult for Verna to accept that Stanley didn't want to make long-term plans. He much preferred waiting to "see how things evolved." But she has learned that this "sometimes seems to work out," and he has learned to "be more of a long-term planner."

Perhaps the greatest gift their relationship brought the community was the affirmation that it was possible to be a cross-cultural family. They were able to talk openly about the experience of parenting Aboriginal children in an urban environment, and to confront some of the very painful struggles their own children faced.

Deep grief and new hope

The boys were extremely close. This made tragedy even more difficult to bear.

One day after supper, Kevin went out bike riding to the new Kildonan Place Shopping Mall with his friend. Shortly after, a phone call from the mall told him that Kevin had fainted and had been taken by ambulance to the hospital. He died later that evening. He had had an undiagnosed congenital heart defect. Stanley and Verna were devastated. Kirk was inconsolable.

Stanley and Verna decided it would be important to adopt another child. After much family discussion and two years later, they requested an eight-year-old boy from the Children's Aid Society of Winnipeg. The CAS responded by saying that they had an eight-year-old boy, but that the child came with two younger sisters, aged three and four.

Stanley was in his seventies and retired. Verna was working full-time, and they agreed that the care of two young pre-school children was too much for Stanley to consider. But the social worker suggested that instead of adopting immediately, they might consider fostering the younger two children. As they discussed this option, they felt that perhaps they had been selfish. They could afford more children; they had the space. They knew the incredible problems faced by young Aboriginal children, and agreed that they would try. A young woman from Fisher River was hired to provide childcare for the younger children until they were in school. Once they were in school, the McKays legally adopted them.

The children were described by the social worker as bright, loveable children, and they were, but they had suffered deep trauma. When they arrived, the McKays' first discovery was that the children insisted they weren't "Indian." Their previous foster mother had assured them they weren't. "You are Native," Verna told them, "like your father and your brother and many others." At first, they refused to believe this; over time, they adjusted.

Verna realized after the adoption that she had met the mother of the children in her work in community ministry. Eventually the children's mother met the girls in the street and introduced herself. They were delighted, but Eric, the boy, refused to see her. Over the years she has become supportive of the children, and the McKays have been open to the children's involvement with their mother, who has been respectful of their family.

Verna comments:

The first ten years following the adoption of the three younger children were busy happy years of adjusting to each other, learning about each other, and working at how we might be a family. But the trauma of the children's earlier years returned, and the next nine years were years of struggle and pain, as each of the three children tried to make sense of what life had been for them, and who they were now. These years were filled with acting out in a variety of ways, followed by weekly visits to treatment centres and family therapists.

We found these years so discouraging, and during this process found little support from the systems that were supposed to be helpful. An example I remember clearly is one family therapy session with the three younger children when all three were angry at us. One of them said, "They're not our family (pointing at us). We three are family!" The therapist made no comment and ended the session. As parents we felt no support in this process. What support we did receive came from an Aboriginal treatment facility.

Also, faith helps one to see beyond the chaos of the moment. One has to see beyond the deep pain; and to know that there is some hope is really important. To watch a child struggle so, and to know that they need to find healing, is very painful. As a family we have had to find ways to both support their growth and yet confront the painful issues.

And Stanley continues:

Hope for me lies in the Christian churches. The church is one body of people with the freedom to address a variety of needs in a variety of ways. Continually my children and I heard comments like, "Why don't you go back where you came from?" and the usual stereotypical cracks about Indians being lazy or drunk. At times like this, I looked to the Christian community for support. The church has made many mistakes, but maybe it is slowly learning to do things with people instead of for them.

Continuing ministry and honours

In 1968, Stanley was relieved of the managerial duties at the lodge so that he could take the position "Worker Among Native People" in the city for nine years. He retired from this position in 1978. Verna had begun working as a liaison worker with the Manitoba Indian Cultural Centre in 1975. In 1977, because the family needed a full-time income, she became a community worker for the North End Community Ministry, and Stanley assumed increased responsibilities at home.

Stanley and Verna have celebrated their thirty-fifth wedding anniversary and Stanley's ninetieth birthday. Both have served in many capacities and received many awards. In 1981, Stanley was honoured to receive the degree Doctor of Sacred Letters from the University of Winnipeg. Verna continued with North End Community Ministry until 1984. During this time she had begun to work with a group of parents who had adopted First Nations children to help them to deal more effectively with the cross-cultural make-up of their families. She has been invited to speak to adoption groups all over Canada and in the United States. For this and other work she too has received an honorary doctorate in Divinity from St. Andrews College in Saskatoon and other awards.

In his eighty-fifth year, Stanley received a surprise. A call came from members of the Eastman family of Riverton, Manitoba, the Icelandic settlement south of Fisher Bay where Stanley had fished for an Icelander. The two women identified themselves as nieces. They indicated that Stanley was the son of their uncle. Stanley was surprised by this revelation, and even more surprised when the women who had identified themselves as his nieces said, "We have all known who you are for some time, and we wanted to meet you." So Stanley learned for the first time the identity of his birth father, an Icelandic fisherman from Riverton. The women presented him with a beautiful hand-knit Icelandic wool sweater, and an invitation to remain in touch. He has since met other members of the family as well, and enjoys ongoing contact.

Both Stanley and Verna have an ability to encourage others in their gifts, and to strengthen their sense of identity. The respect, trust, and honour with which they are both held by the Aboriginal, as well as the non-Aboriginal, community has enabled them to work very effectively to develop cross-cultural understanding. Their lives hold up a vision of hope.

> I really get hung up on dwelling too much on the past, saying, "The white man stole my land," "The church stole my religion," "They won't accept my culture and my medicine," "They spoiled my life." Many of these accusations are justified, but name calling will never change the past. Although we cannot change the past, we can learn from it for the future. Action brings about change. Past experience is a great teacher, but the future is where the opportunity lies, to do something about now.

Stanley has been guided on his way by the spiritual understandings of Aboriginal tradition as well as his deep Christian faith, both nurtured in the community of his childhood. He believes he was fortunate to have experienced childhood in a community rooted in the values of Aboriginal tradition.

ABC Publishing
ANGLICAN BOOK CENTRE

Bridges in Spirituality
First Nations Christian Women Tell Their Stories
Joyce Clouston Carlson and Alf Dumont, editors
Five Elder women tell the stories of their life and, in doing so, teach the deep truths of living. A wonderful resource for homily, reading, storytelling, study, and meditation. Links Aboriginal culture and Christian understanding.
1-55126-063-1 $18.95

Beyond Traplines
Does the Church Really Care?
Towards an Assessment of the Work of the Anglican Church of Canada with Canada's Native People
Charles E. Hendry
A synopsis of the Report of the Royal Commissin on Aboriginal Peoples 1996 and a description of the social conditions and obstacles faced by Aboriginal peoples of Canada.
1-55126-227-4 $14.95

All Who Minister
New Ways of Serving God's People
Maylanne Maybee, editor
These first-hand stories from the frontiers of alternative ministry, and ground-breaking articles on the theology of ministry, offer inspiring models and rationales for all who minister — whether in a venerable tradition or on the forefront of change. Exciting and creative!
1-55126-341-6 $24.95

Vision Quest
Native Spirituality and the Church in Canada
Janet Hodgson and Jay Kothare
This study surveys the involvement of the mainline Christian churches with Canada's Native peoples. The analysis and reflection are probing and soul-searching; the varied sources arise from a diversity of Christian traditions.
0-921846-04-5 $26.95

The Journey
Stories and Prayers for the Christian Year from People of the First Nations
Joyce Clouston Carlson, editor
From the high Arctic to the lush forests of southern Ontario, the spiritual journey of a people emerges. These stories from an oral literary tradition are a gift from people of the First Nations who seek to share their stories more widely with each other and within the context of the larger Christian community.
0-921846-40-1 $11.99

Available from your local bookstore or

Anglican Book Centre
416-924-1332
toll-free 1-800-268-1168
email: abc@national.anglican.ca
Internet: www.abcpublishing.com